First World War
and Army of Occupation
War Diary
France, Belgium and Germany

36 DIVISION
Headquarters, Branches and Services
Royal Army Ordnance Corps
Deputy Assistant Director Ordnance Services
30 September 1915 - 30 May 1919

WO95/2495/2

The Naval & Military Press Ltd
www.nmarchive.com
Published in association with The National Archives

Published by

The Naval & Military Press Ltd

Unit 10 Ridgewood Industrial Park,

Uckfield, East Sussex,

TN22 5QE England

Tel: +44 (0) 1825 749494

www.naval-military-press.com

www.nmarchive.com

This diary has been reprinted in facsimile from the original. Any imperfections are inevitably reproduced and the quality may fall short of modern type and cartographic standards.

© **Crown Copyright**
Images reproduced by permission of The National Archives, London, England, 2015.

Contents

Document type	Place/Title	Date From	Date To
Heading	WO95/2495/2		
Heading	36th Division Divl Troops D.A. Dir. Ordnance Services Oct 1915-May 1919		
Heading	D.A.D.D. 36th Div. Vol. I II III Oct 15 Nov May 19 DE		
Heading	War. Diary D.A.D.O.S. 36th Division		
War Diary	Boulogne	30/09/1915	01/10/1915
War Diary	Flesselles	01/10/1915	21/10/1915
War Diary	Domart	22/10/1915	29/11/1915
War Diary	Pont. Remy	30/11/1915	03/01/1916
War Diary	Pont Remy	01/01/1916	02/01/1916
War Diary	Domart	04/01/1916	18/01/1916
War Diary	Bernaville	19/01/1916	06/02/1916
War Diary	Auchey	07/02/1916	22/02/1916
War Diary	Ascheux	23/02/1916	03/04/1916
War Diary	Harponville	04/04/1916	21/04/1916
War Diary	Hedauville	22/04/1916	02/07/1916
War Diary	Hedauville	01/08/1916	02/08/1916
War Diary	Hedauville	03/07/1916	05/07/1916
War Diary	Rubempre	06/07/1916	06/07/1916
War Diary	Hedauville	03/07/1916	05/07/1916
War Diary	Rubempre	06/07/1916	11/07/1916
War Diary	Rubempre	07/07/1916	11/07/1916
War Diary	Tilques	12/07/1916	16/07/1916
War Diary	Tilques	12/07/1916	21/07/1916
War Diary	Tilques	17/07/1916	21/07/1916
War Diary	Esquelbecq	22/07/1916	23/07/1916
War Diary	Bailleul (Farm)	24/07/1916	26/07/1916
War Diary	Esquelbecq	22/07/1916	23/07/1916
War Diary	Bailleul (Farm)	24/07/1916	26/07/1916
War Diary	Bailleul	27/07/1916	31/07/1916
War Diary	B I Central	01/08/1916	31/10/1916
War Diary	B I Central (De Seule)	01/11/1916	13/11/1916
War Diary	B I Central	14/11/1916	19/01/1917
War Diary	De Seule	20/01/1917	18/03/1917
War Diary	Hill Farm Sheet 28 S.9.B. Central	19/03/1917	28/03/1917
War Diary	Hill Farm	28/03/1917	15/04/1917
War Diary	Hill Farm Sheet 28 S.9.b.6.5	16/04/1917	04/05/1917
War Diary	Hill Farm	05/05/1917	09/05/1917
War Diary	Hill Farm Sheet 28 S.9. b. Central	10/05/1917	18/05/1917
War Diary	Hill Farm S.9.b. Cen	19/05/1917	22/05/1917
War Diary	Hill Farm	23/05/1917	05/06/1917
War Diary	Hille	05/06/1917	07/06/1917
War Diary	Hille Farm	08/06/1917	14/06/1917
War Diary	Hille Farm Sheet 28 S.9.b Central	15/06/1917	17/06/1917
War Diary	Hille Farm	18/06/1917	30/06/1917
War Diary	Merris	01/07/1917	07/07/1917
War Diary	Wizernes	08/07/1917	16/07/1917
War Diary	Wizernes (Hazebrouck 5a)	17/07/1917	25/07/1917
War Diary	Winnezele Sheet 27 J.17.A.5.6	26/07/1917	27/07/1917

War Diary	Winnezeele	28/07/1917	30/07/1917
War Diary	Poperinghe	31/07/1917	06/08/1917
War Diary	Ten Elms Camp	07/08/1917	12/08/1917
War Diary	Ten Elms Camp A25d.5.3	13/08/1917	17/08/1917
War Diary	Winnezeele	18/08/1917	24/08/1917
War Diary	Sheet 57c O.21.d.1.4	24/08/1917	29/08/1917
War Diary	Sheet 57c O.23.d.54	30/08/1917	31/08/1917
War Diary	Bus	01/09/1917	06/10/1917
War Diary	Bus (Somme)	07/10/1917	30/11/1917
War Diary	Bus (Somme)	01/11/1917	11/11/1917
War Diary	Ytres (Somme)	12/11/1917	18/11/1917
War Diary	Ytres	19/11/1917	26/11/1917
War Diary	Bus	27/11/1917	30/11/1917
War Diary	Achiet-Le-Petit	01/12/1917	01/12/1917
War Diary	Bus	02/12/1917	05/12/1917
War Diary	Sorel	06/12/1917	08/12/1917
War Diary	Sorel Le Grand	09/12/1917	16/12/1917
War Diary	Lucheux	17/12/1917	28/12/1917
War Diary	Corbie	29/12/1917	07/01/1918
War Diary	Harbonnieres	08/01/1918	15/01/1918
War Diary	Ollezy	16/01/1918	21/03/1918
War Diary	Trenches	22/03/1918	22/03/1918
War Diary	Beaulieu	23/03/1918	23/03/1918
War Diary	Guerbigny	24/03/1918	25/03/1918
War Diary	Grivesnes	26/03/1918	26/03/1918
War Diary	Chirmont	27/03/1918	27/03/1918
War Diary	Essetaux	28/03/1918	28/03/1918
War Diary	Wailly	29/03/1918	29/03/1918
War Diary	Gamaches	30/03/1918	03/04/1918
War Diary	Peselhoek	04/04/1918	05/04/1918
War Diary	Ten Elms	06/04/1918	07/04/1918
War Diary	Seige Camp	08/04/1918	12/04/1918
War Diary	Dragon Camp	13/04/1918	14/05/1918
War Diary	Nr Dragon Camp	15/05/1918	21/05/1918
War Diary	Nr Dragon Camp	22/04/1918	26/05/1918
War Diary	Proven	27/05/1918	28/05/1918
War Diary	La Lovie	29/04/1918	09/05/1918
War Diary	Couthove Chateau	09/05/1918	21/05/1918
War Diary	Dragon Camp	22/05/1918	02/06/1918
War Diary	Couthove	03/06/1918	30/06/1918
War Diary	Couthove Chat	01/07/1918	03/07/1918
War Diary	Cassel	04/07/1918	09/07/1918
War Diary	Terdeghem	10/07/1918	01/09/1918
War Diary	St Silvestre Cappel	02/09/1918	02/09/1918
War Diary	Montdes Caps	03/09/1918	06/09/1918
War Diary	St Lane Cappel	07/09/1918	22/09/1918
War Diary	St. Jan. Ter Beizen	23/09/1918	27/09/1918
War Diary	Vogeltje	28/09/1918	30/09/1918
War Diary	Ypres	01/10/1918	02/10/1918
War Diary	St	03/10/1918	15/10/1918
War Diary	Becelaere	16/10/1918	16/10/1918
War Diary	Ledeghem	17/10/1918	18/10/1918
War Diary	Winkel St Eloi	19/10/1918	19/10/1918
War Diary	Lendelade	20/10/1918	24/10/1918
War Diary	Hulste	25/10/1918	28/10/1918
War Diary	Belleghem	29/10/1918	03/11/1918

War Diary   Mouscron   04/11/1918   30/05/1919

W0951 2495/2

36TH DIVISION
DIVL TROOPS

D.A.DIR. ORDNANCE SERVICES
OCT 1915-MAY 1919

Supp. 36th Div.
Vol. I II III

Oct. 15
May 19

War Diary

D.A.D.O.S.
36th Division

Army Form C. 2118.

19 Divn. from
30.9.15. to. 24.12.15.

WAR DIARY
or
INTELLIGENCE SUMMARY.
(Erase heading not required.)

Instructions regarding War Diaries and Intelligence Summaries are contained in F. S. Regs., Part II. and the Staff Manual respectively. Title pages will be prepared in manuscript.

Place	Date	Hour	Summary of Events and Information	Remarks and references to Appendices
	1915			
Boulogne	30-9	6 p.m.	Arrived from England.	
	1-10	-	Started for Headquarters and reported to D.D.O.S, who issued instructions re Stores etc.	
Flixecourt	"	-	Returns from Headquarters. Stayed in station.	
	2-10	-	Visited Railhead. D.D.O.S. also visited Flixecourt re Stores. Spoke to Staff-Captain, R.A. re same and list will be furnished as soon as possible.	
	3-10	-	Called to Office of D.O.S. - instructions re Smoke Helmets. – 2 per man and one spare for Divl Reserve. Questioned re Guns etc.	
	4-10	-	Made out instructions for Brigade transport Officers. Saw AA and QMG re smoke helmets etc., for Divisional Orders.	
	5-10	-	Made arrangements for Boots and Ammunition shop. Talks over arrangements for Shoemaking, tanning and tailors shop. G.O.C. decided that latter not necessary, and that only former should be formed.	

Army Form C. 2118.

WAR DIARY
or
INTELLIGENCE SUMMARY.
(Erase heading not required.)

Place	Date	Hour	Summary of Events and Information	Remarks and references to Appendices
	1915			
FLESSELLES	6.10.	—	Visited 1st Division D.A.D.O.S. re Shops. and Armourers Shop. Talked over arrangements for Shoemakers, Farriers and Tailors Shops. Looked at Records in their Office and talked things over generally as regards working in Division	
"	7.10.	—	Ordered 9 Armourers in to work in Shops. Orders issued for Units to return all Rifles, Bayonets etc. requiring repair. Visited 1/1st and 1/3rd Brigades R.F.A. Discovered they had places for Forges the where shoeing was being carried out. Saw Lt. Cole who desired not to concentrate but to work at Forges already there.	
"	8.10.	—	Again visited 13th Brigade re Inputs.	
"	9.10.	—	Received 100 francs for Repair. Visited 16th R.F.A. re helmets — some of which I examined.	
"	10.10.	—	Wagon for 252 Company arrived (J.S.) Purchases 12 Lamps for Headquarters at AMIENS. Visited 108th Field Ambulance	

Army Form C. 2118.

3/

WAR DIARY
or
INTELLIGENCE SUMMARY.
(Erase heading not required.)

Place	Date	Hour	Summary of Events and Information	Remarks and references to Appendices
FLESSELLES	1915 10-10	—	re Bakers Carts (Damaged filler), also 11th Bn. Irish Rifles, and 9th Bn. Inniskilling Fusrs.	
"	11-10	—	Visited 11th Bn. Inniskilling Fusiliers; 1/3rd Ammunition Column; No. 4 Company A.S.C.; 2nd. Supply Column No. 2 Company, A.S.C. 14th Bn. Irish Rifles, 110th Fd Amber. Had Out Orders issued re. drawing Stores as Unit details on this Front.	
"	12-10	—	Visited 9th Bn. Irish Fusiliers, also 11th Inniskilling Fusrs. Indent received from 15th Brigade for Drawings Field. Envelopes marked B.E.F. One that nets for 2 pts Col. Colza for Lamps electric signalling.	
"	13-10	—	Visited 11th Division – Forms and following information:– Goggles issued for R.A. at rate of 24 per Batty, ride 6.J. F.6667/431 of. 10/15. Brushes sweeping 27° new only shown here 47° Forms 27° and Brushes scrubbing Hand. 27° new rate DDOS G.H.Q. 303 of 24/4/15 and S.E.O. 75 of 28/4/15	

1577 Wt.W10791/1773 500,000 1/15 D. D. & L. A.D.S.S./Forms/C. 2118.

WAR DIARY
or
INTELLIGENCE SUMMARY.
(Erase heading not required.)

Army Form C. 2118.

Place	Date	Hour	Summary of Events and Information	Remarks and references to Appendices
FLESSELLES	13.10	—	Unusual Grazier are handed over to General Staff. Took Lt. Cordr. Sutton to 4th. Division owing to transfer of Brigades. Arranged re. handing over of blankets etc.	
"	14.10	—	Arranged with Adjt. 14th re. drawings etc. for alteration of Basket anns. Visited 1/13rd 1/1st 1/14th and Divisional Ammunition Column. Latter are in possession of long rifles.	
"	15.10	—	Visited 13th R. Irish Rifles re. Lithe Helmets required to replace "it" — noted also Divl Supply Column, and Ammn Park who are both in possession of Reynolds.	
"	16.10	—	After purchasing troughs, iodine, or canvas for covers for 6th F.S. Inniskilling Dragoons and lamps at Amiens returned to Headquarters	
"	17.10	—	Visited office of D.D.O.S. who was out. Saw Lt. Barclay re. issue of Winter Caps, Clothing for Cooks, etc. No more issues prior to Helmet to be supplied	
"	18.10 19.10 20.10	—	Collection of Rifles from Divl. Train. Supply Column, etc.	

Army Form C. 2118.

WAR DIARY
or
INTELLIGENCE SUMMARY.
(Erase heading not required.)

Instructions regarding War Diaries and Intelligence Summaries are contained in F.S. Regs., Part II. and the Staff Manual respectively. Title pages will be prepared in manuscript.

Place	Date	Hour	Summary of Events and Information	Remarks and references to Appendices
	1915			
LESSELLES	21-10	—	Moved to Domart. Settled.	
DOMART	22-10	—	Ordered to Rep. 100 tents. Sent truck back to Reg. Station who has plenty. If any more required ask D.D.O.S. Received Duplicate copy of voucher from T.O.O. Down for 173rd Blw. Received Rifles from "A" Inf. Park.	
"	23-10	—	Purchased 12 Brooms for A.P.M. who required same urgently for prisoners.	
"	24-10 25-10 26-10	—	Visited all units of 109th Brigade and arranged for any urgent Stores to be sent to them prior to going up.	
"	27-10	—	Received 3 truck loads of Sun waterproofs and distributed to Units.	
"	28-10 and 29-10	—	Office — Large consignment of Winter Clothing.	
"	30-10	—	Visited 15th Rl. Irish Fusiliers Rifles re. Travelling Kitchens. Found that instead of requiring 2 new Kitchens, they only wanted one repaired, which was ordered to W.T. urgently.	
"	1-11	—	Arranged re. Indents with Major Mearns — also Special Store.	
"	2-11	—	Office.	

WAR DIARY or INTELLIGENCE SUMMARY

Army Form C. 2118.

Place	Date	Hour	Summary of Events and Information	Remarks and references to Appendices
DOMART	3-11	—	Conference at Headquarters. 3rd Army re Surplus Stores of 2 Divisions leaving. Obtained among other items 750 Blicks, Latrine. Reported to A.A.Q.M.G. Sent 50 Frame Books to 11th R. Inniskilling Inns. urgent. Then took of Transport arrived they had moved. He delivered them at Car Railhead and Office. Sent Gun Books to 16th Bn. Irish Rifles.	
"	4-11	—		
"	5-11	—	3 trucks in. Arranged other items 710 Gun Books deliveries to 11th Bn. Inniskilling Ins. Arranged other items, Lorry 1 sent to V. Bretonneux for Latrine Buckets and orders to deliver to Headquarters of Brigades. He delivered to 108th and 109th Bdes, and Evacuated Cars. Looked up at night consignment for 122nd and 150th Bde. R.E. also Headquarters and 16th R.I.R. Thanks 11th Bn. Inniskilling Ins. 12th & 13th R. Ir. Rifles	
"	6-11	—	re Special Stores, i.e. No. of R.E. in possession, Rifle Sights and Machine Gun Special Stores. Sent lince to AMIEN to purchase Oil Stores, Bought.	

WAR DIARY or INTELLIGENCE SUMMARY

Army Form C. 2118.

Place	Date	Hour	Summary of Events and Information	Remarks and references to Appendices
DOMART	6-11 1915		cap at 29/. and 5 at 35/. Left Stephens at BEAUVAL workshops. 3 Lorries to be rails to each Field Ambulance.	
"	7-11		Two or three questions on Boots, notably 108th Bde.- 11th R.I.R. Visited Headquarters 109th Brigade re Kitchens and cots. Asked Brigade major to send in 3 of each at a time. Conversation with General Hickman re Boots and Brigade W.O. Arranged to transfer a few number from 9th Rl Innskilling Fusrs, and send over to 10th and 11th (do), also a few for 11th Rl Irish Rifles. Sent Lorries off for these, also arranged for 2 Kitchens (9th Rl Innskilling Fusrs) to be sent by same Lorries from 10 A.A.Q.M.G. re T.O. for Brigade, and arranged to send Lieut. Corder. Sellar.	
"	8-11		4 Ammunition arrived for duty in Ammunition Dept. Lorry sent to Flixecourt. Truck arrived, Detail Iron, Gloves, Flints, etc.,	

WAR DIARY or INTELLIGENCE SUMMARY

Army Form C. 2118.

Place	Date	Hour	Summary of Events and Information	Remarks and references to Appendices
DOMART	1915 9-11	-	Wired for Base to send urgently on Sunday 1000 pairs Boots, but truck did not arrive. Tried Regulating Sta. Abbeville - no reply. Went to AMIENS to try Lorries (36) 8 for each Brigade, 2 L.Qr.R.A, 2 each for Brigade H.Qr; Visited Headquarters 3rd Army. 1 Lorry to Flesselles, one to V. Bretonneux. 1 to Hd.Qr. 3rd Army Troops.	
"	10-11	-	1 Lorry Flesselles. Visited Cashier - Office - 1 Lorry Flesselles (800 francs)	
"	11-11	-	Visited 9th R.L. Snan, and 14th R. Lish Rifles - Question re Tube Helmets and Boots. Lorries 9th R.L.O. to draw Supplies of S.A.A. being returned by Field Ambulances from Casualties and A.D.M.S. and arranged that same should be taken direct to Ammn Sub Park. Visits 1/3 Bde R.F.A. Units, and B57 & C57 Bhys. Lorry to 1/3 Bde	
"	12-11	-		
"	13-11	-	with Greatcoats. Drew clothing urgently required by B & C/57 Bhys on	

1577 Wt.W10791/1773 500,000 1/15 D.D.& L. A.D.S.S./Forms/C. 2118.

WAR DIARY
or
INTELLIGENCE SUMMARY.

Army Form C. 2118.

2

Place	Date	Hour	Summary of Events and Information	Remarks and references to Appendices
DOMART	1915 13-11	—	Mobilization for service elsewhere. Wires 3rd Army for instructions from whom to draw. Such Gum Boots to be returned meantime and reissue to Infantry Units when going into action. Visited 11th and 16th Rl. Irish Rifles.	
"	14-11	—	Pressing demands for Gum Boots anki. See again wires to expedite despatch. Local purchase of Gum Firing etc. at Amiens.	
"	15-11	—	Visited 1/2nd Bde. R.F.A. and 1/4 - 1/5th Bdys. Shortage of nose bags. Only 100 received from Base out of 2000 demanded.	
"	16-11	—	Office. Lorry to 4th Division with Gum Boots for 13th and 13th Rl Irish Rifles. Visited 9th and 10th Rl. Inniskilling Fusrs.	
"	17-11	—	Lorry to 109th Brigade with Gum Boots. Purchase of Lamps at Amiens for H.Q. Cars. also Brushes, etc. brooms etc.	

Army Form C. 2118.

WAR DIARY
or
INTELLIGENCE SUMMARY.
(Erase heading not required.)

Instructions regarding War Diaries and Intelligence Summaries are contained in F. S. Regs., Part II. and the Staff Manual respectively. Title pages will be prepared in manuscript.

Place	Date	Hour	Summary of Events and Information	Remarks and references to Appendices
DOMART	18.11.'15	—	Lorry to 37th Division to collect Caps Knackisock and Vest Woollen to complete B & C 57 Bde. Units notified owing to shortage of Nose Bags all repairable ones should be returned. Visited Units of 109th Brigade. Supply of Books received on distribution	
"	19.11	—	Office. Supply of Books received on distribution issues. Lorry to 4th Division with 120 Rugs horse. Visited Amiens and purchased Sandy Brushes lorry to 48th Division with Spares for 12th and 13th Fd. Amb. All Horse Lorst of Instruction to be sent to 3rd Army troops.	
"	20.11	—	Rifles. All Horse for School of Instruction to be sent to 3rd Army troops	
"	21.11	—	Visited 1/1st Brigade R.F.A. and 11-1/2 Bde. Lorry to Doms Loges. Truck 206/4 advised from Base 6/11 still no trace. Wired Traffic 3rd Army. Explains supply of Jerkins leather received. Wired 3rd Army for	

Army Form C. 2118.

WAR DIARY
or
INTELLIGENCE SUMMARY.
(Erase heading not required.)

Instructions regarding War Diaries and Intelligence Summaries are contained in F. S. Regs., Part II and the Staff Manual respectively. Title pages will be prepared in manuscript.

Place	Date	Hour	Summary of Events and Information	Remarks and references to Appendices
	11/15			
DOMART	21-11	-	Instructions as to Disposal.	
"	22-11	-	Lorry to 48th Division with Lewis gun for 12th & 13th Irish Rifles. Lewis Gun received and issued to 2 Bn Lancashire Fusiliers for instructional purposes.	
"	23-11	-	Office. Visited 1/1st Brigade R.F.A. and 1/3 Bty also 9th and 10th R. Inniskilling Fus.	
"	24-11	-	Sent to Amiens and purchases Lamps for Artillery also Oil Stoves. Visited 11th and 18th R. Irish Rifles and 9th R. Irish Fusiliers. Ordered tanks carts of 12th Brigade units into Ordnance Travelling Workshops for conversion.	
"	25-11	-	Visited 1/5 So. Lancs Regt., 1st Kings Own and 14th Royal Irish Rifles. Checked Indents and Examined Stores urgently required. Lieutenant H. Hicks Glanvill Fasenets from Base and Lieut C.A. Trackenye arrived from Base and reported for duty	

WAR DIARY or INTELLIGENCE SUMMARY

Army Form C. 2118.

Place	Date	Hour	Summary of Events and Information	Remarks and references to Appendices
DOMART	1915 26-11	—	P.P.C.L.I. Leave Division. Leave stock of Shirts, Socks and Drawers for Dist. Baths received and distributed. Purchased Sundry at Amiens urgently required by Units and not available from Base. Trucks 172 Brigade R.F.A. and Batteries and 14th Bn Irish Rifles.	
"	27-11	—	Congestion of Stores in Dumps. Lorry sent to 16th Bn Irish Rifles. Other Units asked to draw early Local purchase at Ally aire Somme of Nose Bags Office Vests woollen not available from Base. 15,000 Shirts demanded in lieu as two indents on Trasten 2nd Lancashire Fusiliers and Divl Supply Column — clothes Labels and Lantens Stores urgently required.	
"	28-11	—		
"	29-11	—	Moves to Pont Remy — Office and General routine work at Dump now at Ally &c and clothn	

Army Form C. 2118.

13

WAR DIARY
or
INTELLIGENCE SUMMARY.
(Erase heading not required.)

Place	Date	Hour	Summary of Events and Information	Remarks and references to Appendices
PONT REMY	1915 30.11	—	Lorries Base to and Trucks again on Wednesday to and failured. Consignment of Blankets received to complete 2 per man, and distributed to Units. Office.	
"	1-12	—	1270 Endaycomb fur, and 1900 Perkins leather knoted over to 30th Division. Visited Armourers Shop. Laminis Shop & Shoemakers Shop. Purchased grinding at Abbeville - urgently required.	
"	2-12	—	Base again. Received for supply of towels. None received by Division since in the country. Visited 11th, 14th and 13th Rifles also 153 Brigade R.F.A. and A.C. and D Btys. re Idents.	
"	3-12	—	Lorries D.A.D.R.T. travells re Truck 246114 not yet received. Visited 15th Brigade R.F.A. also Btys and Ammunition Column. Looked them re Idents and when to draw Stores. - Office work.	

WAR DIARY or INTELLIGENCE SUMMARY

Army Form C. 2118.

Place	Date	Hour	Summary of Events and Information	Remarks and references to Appendices
PONT REMY	1915 4-12	-	Lorry to Div. Supply Column and proceeded onwards to Div. Railhead and Dump.	
"	5-12	-	Proceeded to Abbeville Div. Remounts dept - Office Clothing Store in Ord. Dump, and generally superintending system of issuing. Visited Farrier Shop, Armourers Shop, and Shoemaker Shop, Farrier Shop, Shoemaker and Farriers shops particularly busy and turning out a good supply.	
"	6-12	-	Visited Hd. Qrs. 109th Brigade. 9th, 10th and 11th Royal Inniskilling Fus., Railhead-Dump, Railhead. Visited 12th and 13th Rl. Irish Rifles, and 9th Rl. Irish Fusiliers.	
"	7-12	-	Iris Base Boots in T.93772, not now required. Visited 1/4 Hors (Bde) R.F.A. Question re. Boots sized them to draw. Office.	
"	8-12	-	Visited Field Cashier and drew 500 francs. Proceeded to Abbeville and purchased Luncheons, Lanterns. Office.	

Army Form C. 2118.

WAR DIARY
or
INTELLIGENCE SUMMARY.
(Erase heading not required.)

15

Place	Date	Hour	Summary of Events and Information	Remarks and references to Appendices
PONT-REMY	1915 Dec 10	—	Duration in Lgh Lorries for Euro Gun in possession of 2nd Lanc. Fus. Not in possession.	
"	11	—	of 36th Div. Artillery and instructs him to return all Div. Stores Latrine Buckets Trays etc to Ordnance Dump before leaving Division.	
"	12	—	Proceeds to Abbeville and purchased towels &c for 108" to Ailly (for use at Div. Baths) Visits 9th Pl. L. Fus. and Div. Ammunition Column	
"	13	—	Calls at Divisional Workshops. Visits No 1 Coy A.S.C. in possession of 5 Wheels cars to be unserviceable, and asks that to return them to Ord. Travelling Workshops. Visits Headquarters and Hqs of 172 and 173 Brigades R.F.A. Checks Latrine generally and Latrines Bars	
"	14	—	from Bar urgently required. Congestion of Stores at Divisional Dump. Visits wires to Draw Stores immediately. Office and Dump.	

Army Form C. 2118.

WAR DIARY
or
INTELLIGENCE SUMMARY.
(Erase heading not required.)

Place	Date	Hour	Summary of Events and Information	Remarks and references to Appendices
PONT REMY	15.12	—	Proceeds to Abbeville, and purchases sundry urgently required for Divl. Shoemaker Shop. Visits 153 Brigade R.F.A, R.B. Bty. and Ammunition Column.	
"	16.12	—	Purchases sundry at Abbeville. Supply of this is not available from base meantime and is very urgently required by Units. Visits 172nd Brigade R.F.A. also Batteries and A. Column.	
"	17.12	—	Office – Visits 48th Mobile Veterinary Section, and Units of 12th Brigade. Checks their Lands, and Lasserns all outstanding items. Question re Towels Road. Again Lasserns from Base.	
"	18.12	—	Visited 30th Divisional tailors. Tells at 108th Brigade. Sundry very urgently required by their instructs them to Lass sent from Divnl. Tums 3d Army re. Ord:nance Refreshers for Killeas.	
"	19.12	—	Large consignment of Stores for 109th Bde. awaiting removal at Divnl. Hastened to Divnl. Office.	

WAR DIARY or INTELLIGENCE SUMMARY

Army Form C. 2118.

Place	Date	Hour	Summary of Events and Information	Remarks and references to Appendices
PONT REMY	1915 20-12	—	Instructed Units of 108th Brigade to send 1 Tool Cart each to Ordnance Landing Workshops D.M.A.R.T for conversion. Visited 10th D.A.C. who promised to send in a quantity of old Horse shoes to Farrier Depot. Question from 10th A. Smithling Train re Spare Iron Cart. Visited F.S. Gr. 15th Brigade R.F.A. also 9th and 11th R. Louis.	
"	21-12	"	Train clothing arrived for Artillery Dis. Batts. Instructed 12th Brigade Units to send Tool Carts to Gas. Workshops for conversion on the 22nd. Railhead Supply re Purchased supply of Lindsay at Abbeville, also Forge for issue to 108th Brigade H.Q.G.C. lorries 3rd Army for 122 Rugs Stores, and 8 Coats. S.L. to complete. Visited Div. A.E. Quachon re Wagon G.S. demands from Base that not in possession. Urgent Demands received from Units.	
"	22-12	"	Div. Artillery for Trayers and Latrine Buckets. Lorries to 3rd Army for Instructions re supply.	

WAR DIARY or INTELLIGENCE SUMMARY

Place	Date	Hour	Summary of Events and Information	Remarks and references to Appendices
PONT REMY	23-12 1915	—	Railhead. Instructed several Units to send books & cards to S.O. to for conversion. Lines move of Capt Bunnell A.O.D. Visited Field Cashier. Purchased sundry at Abbeville. Am Sub Pk now administered by Corps troops	
"	24-12	—		
"	25-12	—	Visited 251-253 Coys A.S.C. re question of brake block. Railhead Supply and General routine. Move of 82nd, 96th and 104th French Provinces B.H.Q. No Infantry. Visited 1/5 South Lancs, 2nd Lancs Fus. and 11th, 12th and 13th Bn. Liverpool Rifles.	
"	26-12	—		
"	27-12	—	Purchased Sundry at Abbeville for Divl. Showerly Shop. Visited 1/1 West Ride R.F.A. and 9th 10th and 11th Bn. Lancs Fus.	
"	28-12	—	53rd Divl. Artillery from Division from 32nd Divn. visited 12th Bn. Liverpool Rifles. Railhead Supply & General work.	

WAR DIARY
INTELLIGENCE SUMMARY

Army Form C. 2118.

Place	Date	Hour	Summary of Events and Information	Remarks and references to Appendices
PONT REMY	1915. 29.12	—	Purchases Sunday at Albeville for Divl. Remounts Dept. Visited 11th Field Bde R.F.A and 11th Fd. Ambce Suar.	
"	30.12	—	Visited 1 Coy A.S.C. re. Wheels. Instructed them to return same to A.O.D. Workshops Dallies at Headquarters Field Artillery. Purchases urgently required by Water Supl. Latrine Buckets urgently required by Water Supl Artillery. Purchases Sunday and Hot Water at Abbeville. Visited 172nd Field Bde.	
"	31.12	—		
"	1916 1.1	—	Visited 173 Bde. R.F.A. 11th Fd. Ambce Suar. and 1 King Own Regt. - Ridsdale - and General Routine work.	
"	2.1	—	Tried Regtl Prison Abbeville to tales truck and Sunday and reconnigre to new Railhead Venters 16th Fd. Irish Rifles & 3rd Fd. Ambce Suar.	
"	3.1	—	Proceed to DONART. called at Hobib Bde R.F.A Officers	

Army Form C. 2118.

WAR DIARY Jan. 1st 1916. to Feb. 29th inclusive
or
INTELLIGENCE SUMMARY.
(Erase heading not required.)

(19)

Instructions regarding War Diaries and Intelligence Summaries are contained in F. S. Regs., Part II. and the Staff Manual respectively. Title pages will be prepared in manuscript.

Place	Date	Hour	Summary of Events and Information	Remarks and references to Appendices
			To Dec. 31st 1915. – already rendered.	
Pont REMY.	1916 Jan. 1	–	Visited 173rd Brigade R.F.A., 11th R. Innis. Fus. and 1st Kings Own Regt. question re. shortage of grindery. The supply at present coming from base is inadequate, and provision is only being kept up by local purchase. Visited Falkins Dump and general routine work.	
do	2	–	Going to impending move to another area, was regarding Lieut. Attiwill to talk this until Tuesday and re-consign to new billets. Visited 16th Rl. Irish Rifles and 9th R. Innis. Fus., called at Divl. workshops. Everything going satisfactory.	

Army Form C. 2118.

WAR DIARY
or
INTELLIGENCE SUMMARY.
(Erase heading not required.)

Place	Date	Hour	Summary of Events and Information	Remarks and references to Appendices
DOMART	1916			
	4-1		Tested Headquarters field Artillery. Complete them to scale in S1098 before authorities for overseas. Establishment copy herewith not rec'd. from 32nd Divn. Enclosed. Visited Machine Gun R.F.A. 1/2 Field Bde. 1/4 14th Rl. Irish Rifles. Railhead Ammn. Column and Dump	
"	5-1			
"	6-1		Move of 15 & 16 Lanc. Regt. to 55th Division 55th D.A.C. 1st Kings Own Regt. 2nd Lanc. Regt. 2nd East Office & general routine work	
"	7-1		Visited 109 Fd Field Ambs. Lewis Dragoons and 9th Rl. Irish Fus. - Dump office	
"	8-1		Purchased Rat Nails at Athville to Girl Guze - Marker shop. Visited 172 Brigade R.F.A. Junction in Nose Bags, Called at 16 H.A.R. Visited 30 Division. - Office Railhead & Dump	
"	9-1			

War Diary / Intelligence Summary

Army Form C. 2118. (21)

Place	Date	Hour	Summary of Events and Information	Remarks and references to Appendices
DOMART	10-1-1916	—	Instructed 2nd Glamorgan Bty. to draw tanks & carts from Railhead. Thanks 1st Monmouth Bty. at Kelamorgan Bty. & 53rd D.A.C. question re Rly horse for 53 D.A.C. — Not to be withdrawn.	
"	11-1	—	Sent to 46 - 47 and 18 Division to read Rifles for issue to 53rd Divl. R.A. Thanks & 300 LIII Bde.	
"	12-1	—	Called & saw H.Q. Coy. Divl. Train, 14 R.G. Rifles 9 R.I. Line and 11th Divnl. Train, A.S.C. question re Brake Block.	
"	13-1	—	Instructed Units to send Tanks Carts to S.O.2. for conversion. Purchased Nose bags at Amiens.	
"	14-1	—	Issued Chlorine Tube Testing case — & an empty tube Case. 1 set of 51 items issued to complete Division. Purchased nose bags at Abbeville.	
"	15-1	—	At Tanks cart and to S.O.M. for conversion. Office —	

Army Form C. 2118.

WAR DIARY
or
INTELLIGENCE SUMMARY.
(Erase heading not required.)

22

Place	Date	Hour	Summary of Events and Information	Remarks and references to Appendices
	1916			
DOMART	16-1	—	Visited H.Q. 108 Bde, 9th R.I. Fus. 11th, 12th and 13th R. Irish Rifles. Dumps general office work.	
"	17-1	—	Purchased Sundry 2 Horse Sledge at Amiens. Called at 172 Brigade H.Q. and Am. Column 1st Gun Bty. and to Field Ambce.	
"	18-1	—	Moved to Bernaville. Visited 121 Field Coy R.E. re hire article (wounerreife) Lorriched came to be sent to I.O.M. Called and went over orders for large demands by 9 R.I. Fus.	
BERNAVILLE	19-1	—	Purchased tables + Hot rails at Abbeville. Visited 37 and 48th Divisions.	
"	20-1	—	47 Lewis Guns received and distributed to units. Bought 3 hammer sledge + at Abbeville for fuel Lorries stop office. Rations Dump.	
"	21-1	—	Visited 15th Bde R.F.A. 10th Irvin Fras. and 12 R.I.R. re Sundry General Office work and Dump.	

Army Form C. 2118.

WAR DIARY
or
INTELLIGENCE SUMMARY.
(Erase heading not required.)

(23)

Place	Date	Hour	Summary of Events and Information	Remarks and references to Appendices
BERNAVILLE	1916 22/1	—	Rothes visited 172 Bde and 36 DAC R.F.A. Question raised by XIV Corps re Gun wads for making Horse Shoes. Only old shoes now in this Division in the reserving. Machine now ready at Travelling Workshops for 12 R.F. B. Scarcity of Nose Bags. 2000 demanded from Base but only 100 received. Increased scale of canvas to make locally.	
"	23-1	—	Withdrew 100 Lanterns tent folding for the Division. Visited 11 Field Bee and + Coy A.S.C.	
"	24-1	—	1st Cambridge Regiment move to 55th Division. Notes Divl Artillery leave the Gun temporarily for training - attached for Ordnance Services to C.O.O. Abbeville.	
"	25-1	—	Lt.Col. Brough, A.O.C, proceeds to Abbeville with Ordnance Lorry. I remain here supervising and take over stores from C.O.O Abbeville for Divl. Artillery.	

WAR DIARY or INTELLIGENCE SUMMARY

Army Form C. 2118.

(24)

Place	Date 1916	Hour	Summary of Events and Information	Remarks and references to Appendices
BERNAVILLE	Jan 26	-	made tent enclosure at Doullens. Visited Candas & Fienvillers and called on 12 Brigade H.Q., 108th Brigade H.Q., 9th Rl Irish Fusiliers and 13th Rl Irish Rifles	
do	27	-	Visited base for Tube Schools (jointly with rubber storage vans to complete 53rd Divl Artillery – Started for but returned having to complete Division to 100 14th Corps main junction at 3rd Army School of Instruction. Replies that O.C. 13 Corps troops had been applying.	
"	28	-	Base query was for 4 additional veterinary surgeons above establishment. – required to replace unavailable. Visited 121st Field Coy. RE at Domesmont. Lorry to Bernaville for Tents.	
"	29	-	Complaints re tents arose being eaten by horses. Charles collar demanded from base to replace. Visited C.O.O. Abbeville re Lorries for Motor Divl Artillery.	
"	30	-	Called & saw A.D.O.S. 17th Corps. D.O.M.A.R.T re new system for working of Divl Supply Officer.	

Army Form C. 2118.

WAR DIARY
or
INTELLIGENCE SUMMARY.
(Erase heading not required.)

(25)

Place	Date	Hour	Summary of Events and Information	Remarks and references to Appendices
BERNAVILLE	1916 Jan 31	—	53rd Div. Artillery now from Rouen for overseas. No 1 Coy. A.S.C. go to Abbeville temporarily. Received from base 1000 pairs Gum Boots Thigh in November.	
do.	Feb 1	—	Special papers and letters kinds over to Artillery. Spent day in attending to urgent clerical work in Office.	
"	2	—	Remainder of 53rd Div. Artillery came for 46th Divn. S.O.W. 14 Motor buses for buses and to be sent in for conversion. Units advised. Railhead visited and Div. Supply.	
"	3	—	Visited units of 109th Brigade re Divine supplies, all satisfied. Motors coming up satisfactory. Made round junctions at Argoeuves.	
"	4 & 5	—	91st, 107 and 9th French Mortar Btys join Division. Office and general clearing up at Group, General visited Railhead, and S.O.W.	

1577 Wt. W10791/1773 500,000 1/15 D. D. & L.   A.D.S.S./Forms/C. 2118.

Army Form C. 2118.

(26)

WAR DIARY
or
INTELLIGENCE SUMMARY.
(Erase heading not required.)

Place	Date 9/16 Feb	Hour	Summary of Events and Information	Remarks and references to Appendices
BERNAVILLE	6	—	109th Railway Company R.E. and 3rd Army Heavy Artillery reserve park Division from 4th Division. 36th Div. Ammunition Column move to 55th Division temporary. Trains now parked at Sirencourt.	
AUCHEL	7	—	Moves to Auchel. Fitted up office, and Div. Workshops.	
do.	8	—	11th Field Btn. R.F.A. move to 16th Division. Issued on "Base" for 1000 batches & solution for the repair of Gum Boots. Trades Unions and purchases Lanterns etc.	
"	9	—	17th Corps raise question re. steel helmets in possession of Division. Already 2837 as supply coming up slowly.	
"	10	—	Visits Boulogne E.O. Office & General routine work. Cells and cars A.S.C. 17 Corps re. local purchases.	
"	11	—	Indents for balance of magazines for Lewis Guns. Purchases paint Brasso &c at Amiens office.	

WAR DIARY or INTELLIGENCE SUMMARY

Army Form C. 2118.

(27)

Place	Date 1916	Hour	Summary of Events and Information	Remarks and references to Appendices
AUCHEL	Feb. 12	—	Underclothing urgently required for Divl. Baths. Erase asked to expedite supply. Thanks Southern and bought Stove arrangers for Divl. Laundries &	
do	13	—	Visited 3rd Army re repairs to vehicles & re cables at 250# Army Troops Coy Rt. - Office. -	
"	14	—	Canvas buckets urgently required by Infantry for carrying bombs, at the rate of 100 per Battalion. To be made locally in Divl. Tailors shops. - Office and general routine work.	
"	15	—	Visited 110th Field Ambulance re trekker cart; 11th and 12th Rl. Irish Rifles, and F.A. Bn. 108th Brigade. Owning to large number of men now attached to Divl. Bonnaire in the capacity of motor lorry drivers & Divl. Workshops the A.S.C. (Supplies) will now ration the detachment direct.	
"	16	—	Spent most of the day at Divl. Dump, clearing up generally and office work.	

Army Form C. 2118.

WAR DIARY
or
INTELLIGENCE SUMMARY.
(Erase heading not required.)

Instructions regarding War Diaries and Intelligence Summaries are contained in F. S. Regs., Part II. and the Staff Manual respectively. Title pages will be prepared in manuscript.

28

Place	Date	Hour	Summary of Events and Information	Remarks and references to Appendices
ACHEUX	1916 FEB. 17	—	Two companies 5th Sherwood Foresters join Division for work on roads &c. Purchased stoves for Officers Rest Station at Forceville.	
do	18	—	Trench Mortar Btys join Division and are allotted as follows 107th Bde - 115th Bty; 108th Bde - 116th Bty; 109th Bde - 119th Bty. Made local purchases at Amiens including wire for Div. Signal Coy. R.E. and lamps for Town Commandant. Finally 1st Indian Field Squadron and 300 British Cavalry arrive at Forceville. left half 5th Trenching Battn. leave Division Depôt for Luchuyt and 91-94 and 107th French Mortar Batteries join 4th Division. Viades 108's J.S. Ambs and HQrs. 107th Brigade.	
"	19	—		
"	20	—	A company of 3rd Labour Battn. join Division and are stationed at Louvencourt; 5 carriages Ambulance, Stretcher, demanded from Base to complete to 20 for Division.	

Army Form C. 2118.

(29)

WAR DIARY
or
INTELLIGENCE SUMMARY.
(Erase heading not required.)

Place	Date 1916	Hour	Summary of Events and Information	Remarks and references to Appendices
AUCHEL	Feb 21	—	Visited Amiens to make local purchases. Bought canvas re urgently required for making nose bags in Divl. Tailors shops to be issued and used by Infantry Battalions for carrying tools. Visited H.Q. 108th Brigade. Ration re. covers for Rifles of the Brigade. The truck Question re. not approved of. Provision of the cover asked for is sanctioned by G.R.O. at a cost of not less than 1 franc each.	
do	22	—	Visited Ratheas and Divl. Dump. Spent rest of morning in attending to office work generally, cables and inspected the Divl. Shoemakers, Armourers & Tailors shops also the Farriers shops at Vaurennes. Visited H.Q. Divl. Artillery. Great shortage of nose bags amongst the Batteries. Tried these for supply to be expedited.	

Place	Date	Hour	Summary of Events and Information	Remarks
Vaulx	Feb 1/2/16 2.3		Snow. 172 Bde and 15"4 Bde Amm. Col's reported that 10th Bde Sery. that rifle covers in the that 10th Bde 3rd Army A1 Reserve had supplied some which were all that were available. I saw Ordnance Officer who agrees that there are not nearly at a mt. of covers available but as they are available the Brigades have been informed of same moving out of the area & further have been informed of same moving out of the area partly and asking r/o further needs still retaining part of covers.	
	2.21		A.A. & Q.M.G. informs me that for Ordinance Stores I must write to 6" Battalion 17th Divn. 1 by A.S.C. from Bapaume for the remainder of the Divn now Reserve. Sent to Division for materials for rifle covers etc.	

Army Form C. 2118.

WAR DIARY
or
INTELLIGENCE SUMMARY.
(Erase heading not required.)

Place	Date	Hour	Summary of Events and Information	Remarks and references to Appendices
Lachine	Dec 25.		Snow had Bordeau to see 17th Corps but they were moving got badly stuck in traffic for 1½ hours French Army on that move with Kindles with snow and getting out lefleurs_ All clear at 10.30 P.M.	
	26		Tailors making food canoes. Saw our new A.D.O.S. at Maiun made like ice with heather snow. Train not in with horseshoes till too late for delivery today.	
	27		Train again late. Went to Doullens & Malhead Sergeant all lorry traffic stopper for "thaw" conveyance all spare transport used in drawing rations from Doullens & some units not able to eat.	

WAR DIARY
INTELLIGENCE SUMMARY.
(Erase heading not required.)

Army Form C. 2118.

(32)

Place	Date 1915	Hour	Summary of Events and Information	Remarks and references to Appendices
Acheux	Feb. 28		At Varennes in afternoon had to wait to walk into time had no cars moving but to walk but first time taken up with cattle trucks this morning this still making drawing of stores delays to 36 Div. Arty. on the move again had one one done up to take over from 4 Div Arty.	
Acheux	29		Any trucks this morning which called well and very little remained - Kelsey belonging to 5 divis. who could get no transport leaves I "thaw" walked to Varennes this week being now sent from Road average stores made up to 2 average from old store 2.2 per diem.	

4 MAR. 1915
D.A.D.O.S.
36th (ULSTER) DIVISION

Mulcahy Lieut
A.D.O.S. 36th Division

WAR DIARY
or
INTELLIGENCE SUMMARY

(Erase heading not required.)

Army Form C. 2118.

Place	Date	Hour	Summary of Events and Information	Remarks and references to Appendices
ASCHEUX	13/1k		This Division from noon today is in X Corps 4th Army. Had wire from base in reply to my demand for canvas for repairing and making of tent, awning. Under what authority are the stores demanded. Had to understand there is a sewing machine was allowed without special authority. Shall require to purchase All situations Clever, lines and report on his forwarded to X Corps. Amiens for local purchase. Much work to do on returns.	
	9/16.		Morning spent in General Routine work. Ind for Artillery makes a great difference and each Quartermaster seem to have had very few stores since they left. Afternoon visiting units	

WAR DIARY
or
INTELLIGENCE SUMMARY.
(Erase heading not required.)

Army Form C. 2118.

Place	Date	Hour	Summary of Events and Information	Remarks and references to Appendices
Acheux	3/3/16		General routine work. Three Trench Mortar Batteries arrived today on from Abbeville for Artillery New Trench Mortar Battery formed 4.2.0. French Mortar Battery A.D.O.S. 10 Corps visited Hd Qrs. 9 mules unfortunately but which so often happens 107th Bde taken over mules from 109th Bde tonight.	
	4/3/6		Snowed hard all day. General Routine work, office + dump.	
	6.3/6		Went 1st Corps Hd Qrs. Saw C.E. Pearson A.D.O.S 10th Corps. to Shell dropped near dump evidently firing at Balloon. Several blind Shells. Saw in Gazette that I have Tituler Captain from 1.9.15.	

WAR DIARY
INTELLIGENCE SUMMARY

Place	Date	Hour	Summary of Events and Information	Remarks and references to Appendices
ASCHEUX	6/3/16		Visited 108 Bde very bad morning with snow. General Routine work.	
	7/3/16		A.D.O.S. 10 Corps here to see about Stores and dumps. General Routine work.	
	8/3/16		Very busy morning in Office many Q.M.S. & Artillery Officers in reminders of day General Routine work.	
	9/3/16		A.D.O.S. called and went into everything in morning visited Bethencourt afternoon to see huts of 107 Infty Bde. have not to press A.A.Q.M.G. asks for new slabs units have not to press	

WAR DIARY
or
INTELLIGENCE SUMMARY.

Army Form C. 2118.

Place	Date	Hour	Summary of Events and Information	Remarks and references to Appendices
A.H. Aschéux	10/3		General routine work. Dr. Dowley to see 17th Corps in afternoon about Water Cart for F.E. Coy.	
	11/3		Received notice of move of 3rd Divn. Monument Back from 49th Divn. but no notice of the 2nd Q.M. of the Back. Arrive for local purchase.	
	12/3		Beautiful day. Rode here saw 107th Inf. Bde. at Mailly and Restancourt. A.D.S.S. 16 Corps here but I did not see him.	

WAR DIARY
or
INTELLIGENCE SUMMARY.
(Erase heading not required.)

Army Form C. 2118.

Place	Date	Hour	Summary of Events and Information	Remarks and references to Appendices
ASCHEUX	13/5		General Routine work in morning saw A.D.O.S. in afternoon & went on to AMIENS to obtain ear.	
	14/5		Took advantage of a Car going to Abbeville to go in for remainder of horse bags that were still due and required. A.D.O.S. spent the morning there at the Dump and gave me some very helpful tips as a reward. 2650 cotton drawers came in lieu of shirts, and were returned.	
	15/5		Spent all day seeing Q.M's and Q.M.S. at Dumps and in Office.	
	16/5		17 Foot Carriers arrived from Boullen Railway	
	17/5		Office & General Routine work.	

WAR DIARY
or
INTELLIGENCE SUMMARY

Army Form C. 2118.

Place	Date	Hour	Summary of Events and Information	Remarks and references to Appendices
ASCHEUX	18/3		Spent morning at Dump and Shops. A.D.O.S. here in afternoon and went into everything in Dump. Later went to DOULLENS.	
	19/3		Returning officers at Dump and Shops. In afternoon saw 10g ACM Rte at Hunstrant and 10 Irm In. 11 Inm Jn. 14 R112. beautiful ride. Mine Dump emptying fine and was burned at 7.30 PM. Sent all records of heavy and all stores but few to A.D.O.S. Arrived at 9.30 PM. Burned few returns.	
	20.3		Busy making arrangements for store 15 Inf. Brigade and finding out what was burnt. The fire casualty was very small of the Stores in an concerning the fire only lasted 1/2 hour before the roof fell in. Great credit is due to the men who lost all their private belongings & cearly got out at the Stant, but they made no attempt to save anything but the records.	

WAR DIARY
or
INTELLIGENCE SUMMARY

Army Form C. 2118.

Place	Date	Hour	Summary of Events and Information	Remarks and references to Appendices
ASCHEUX	17/3		and store till he has left to get near this area.	
	18/3		Court of Inquiry sat	
	19/3		General Routine work. Wanted to clean up various effects from a part in temporary pool. Visited units	
	20/3		Visits with a General Routine work. Saw 108 R&e at Engelbelmer	
	21/3		General Routine work visited 356 Towed Reinforcements, Machine Gunners & Louvin and R.A.	

Army Form C. 2118.

WAR DIARY
or
INTELLIGENCE SUMMARY.
(Erase heading not required.)

Instructions regarding War Diaries and Intelligence Summaries are contained in F. S. Regs., Part II and the Staff Manual respectively. Title pages will be prepared in manuscript.

Place	Date	Hour	Summary of Events and Information	Remarks and references to Appendices
ASCHEUX	25/3		Shooting match v General Roules worn.	
	26/3		General Roules worn.	
	27/3		Several lorries to AMIENS of material for repair, helpers of Reams outin to be reassembled on Tuesday. Saw A.D.O.S. at Toutencourt, without fault heavy.	
	28/3		Visited units in Vicinity. Dumps out Stores A.D.O.S. 8th Corps & R.A.O.O.S. 29th Div here in afternoon. Reams assembled and for more detail.	

Army Form C. 2118.

WAR DIARY
or
INTELLIGENCE SUMMARY.
(Erase heading not required.)

Place	Date	Hour	Summary of Events and Information	Remarks and references to Appendices
ASCHEOX	29.3		General Routine work and at Harponville to see, and were arranged for Dump Office and Shops. Shoemakers shop to derive, hope to make better arrangements later.	
	30/3		General Routine work office shops & Dump.	
	31/3		Visiting work Harponville where I hear I am to move.	
	1/4			

WAR DIARY
or
INTELLIGENCE SUMMARY.
(Erase heading not required.)

Army Form C. 2118.

Place	Date	Hour	Summary of Events and Information	Remarks and references to Appendices
	1/4/1[8]		Visiting with General Routine Armies for leave furniture etc.	
	2/4		Moved Armourers shop Shoemakers & Tailors visits with & General Routine Duties.	
	3/4		Tailorsmith Callers on A D O S at Toutencourt visited with Moved Dump & Head Qrs to Harponville.	

WAR DIARY or INTELLIGENCE SUMMARY

Army Form C. 2118.

Place	Date	Hour	Summary of Events and Information	Remarks and references to Appendices
Harbonville	4/4/16		General Routine work in office. Arranged offices after work.	
	5/4/16		Lieut. D. Cavan A.V.C. arrived for instruction in H.Q.H.Q. duties. General Routine work.	
	6/4/16		General Routine work. Pct. O.S. & Copes visited xxDGs & spent some time in office & dump.	
	7/4/16		Visited Abattoir & made local purchase of tallow etc. for enable Tailors shops to complete Small Grenade carriers. Scheme made up on instruction from "E".	
	8/4/16		Scheme made up for Return of Winter Clothing from # Army R.O. & "Corps" allotment of trucks. Instructions to Units issued on R.O. on this & following dates. Arrangement made with R.O.O. Belle Eglise re the Return of this clothing	

WAR DIARY
or
INTELLIGENCE SUMMARY

(Erase heading not required.)

Army Form C. 2118.

Place	Date	Hour	Summary of Events and Information	Remarks and references to Appendices
	9/4/16		Arrangements made at Belle Eglise for receiving the clothing from Huts & collecting from 109 & 16 ourselves owing to distance that would have to be covered by regimental transport. The Bde. & I made 2 my Staff Platoons there(B'S) to give receipts & superintend a fatigue party in sorting, packing in bundles. Sets. to the clothing ready for return to Paris. Remained fully Par. See.	Cartage 18/07 O.7. standards for C/15 36 replace damages clothing & not demand made for pairs or cartridges ammunition inventory
	10/4/16		Return of the Coats commenced in morning. Met Board of Survey of one Captain & subaltern at Belle Eglise & arranged with them for future meetings to inspect & condemn the clothing worn out as unfit for return to Paris. General Routine work in office. Went to Amiens for local purchases. Unable to meet Board.	
	11/4/16		As arranged, away to Sholays & car in the afternoon. General Routine work – saw S.S.O. 2 re: General Garrison. Special items required by Bdes. etc. Visit from A.D.D. & H.Q.R.S.	Issued(?) 21,000 P.H. Helmets Only 500 in Dipol Reserve
	12/4/16		Had experimental work & mortar made in Shoemakers & lot from re-bent bodies, belt hooks & soft slab of leather made into stays turning tools for writ. required by Bde Bombers for throwing Mills hand grenades.	

WAR DIARY
or
INTELLIGENCE SUMMARY
(Erase heading not required.)

Army Form C. 2118.

Place	Date	Hour	Summary of Events and Information	Remarks and references to Appendices
	14/4/16		General Routine work. Sent out work details for that of 108th M.G. Mortar Officer. Capt MacKenzie is attd. D.A.D.O.S. returned from leave.	
	15/4/16		General Routine work in office and at Dump. Drew a lot of tents for tents as we shall be far more crowded in Division and have to be up under canvas and huts to make room. 107/2 T.M.B. joined today.	
	16/4/16		Railhead + visiting units. Number of bicycles in for repair heavy, Hotchkiss steel 1407 wires for for 7th Coys. 7th and T.M.B. vide QMG O/os 290/a 4th.	
	17/4/16		Loose punching point and material for repair. Visited units.	

WAR DIARY
or
INTELLIGENCE SUMMARY.

Army Form C. 2118.

Place	Date	Hour	Summary of Events and Information	Remarks and references to Appendices
Hébuterne	18/4		Arranged new dump at Terrence Shops and killed the accommodation not very good. A.D.O.S. called & saw office dump est. Wired for Box Respirators & P.H.G. Helmets to complete under D.S.S. No. 2609/2/65 11/4/16	
	19/4		Moved dump, visited railhead & Hebuterne Hebuterne. Steel helmets still required to complete est. 1113.	
	20/4		Moved to Hebuterne. Visited 108 Bde & 109 Bde.	
	21/4		Wired for 168 hand carts for Lewis guns, local purchased in Amiens, A.D.O.S. up here.	

WAR DIARY
or
INTELLIGENCE SUMMARY.
(Erase heading not required.)

Army Form C. 2118.

Place	Date	Hour	Summary of Events and Information	Remarks and references to Appendices
Hebuterne	22/4		Sergt Harmsworth A.O.C. moved to XV Corps & Offr Shaw took over his work the relief not having arrived.	
	23/4		10 R. Irish. Fus. Lewis gun reserved out arrived for reserve.	
	24/4		Received Lewis gun for 14 U.R.I.R. which had been destroyed by shell fire.	
	25/4		V36 Heavy T.M.B. is being formed gun = 9.5"	

WAR DIARY
or
INTELLIGENCE SUMMARY

Army Form C. 2118.

Place	Date	Hour	Summary of Events and Information	Remarks and references to Appendices
Hedauville	26/4		Great funerary in Querieux in morning. Divy and General Parker down. Div Cavalry rejoined after a fortnight's training with 2nd Aust C.C. and Hangest & Hornsoy Gen. withdrew.	
	27/4		Visits T.M.B's and saw HS Quartermasters of 108. Inf. Bde. most of the units from now in Div Cyclist returns to Bn Coday after a fortnight's training.	
	28/4		Pallières & Prativillers Two New T.M.B. 240 M.H. to be formed known as V.36 & W.36.	
	29/4		General routine work in office All the trumps and the Qrs made up inprov account. Vickers dump morning & afternoon.	
	30/4			

D.A.D.O.S.
36th Division
MAY & JUNE
Vols 5.6

Army Form C. 2118.

WAR DIARY
or
INTELLIGENCE SUMMARY
(Erase heading not required.)

Instructions regarding War Diaries and Intelligence Summaries are contained in F. S. Regs., Part II. and the Staff Manual respectively. Title Pages will be prepared in manuscript.

Place	Date	Hour	Summary of Events and Information	Remarks and references to Appendices
HEADVILLE	1/5		Intr Gen return sent in. Visited Div Training & 10 P.O.I.R. at Headville wire to feel byline railhead. Rec'd orders to collect special stores for a special purpose some of which must be brought.	
	2/5		Local Purchasing in morning for Hd. Qrs. & in afternoon at Dump. 11/1 T.M.B. is now known as 107/1 T.M.B. rejoined after training. Steel helmets in possession 135·24	
	3/5		General routine work; Railheads + dumps.	
	4/5		Barbed wire (W 2281) orders for distribution of magazine Lewis gun. General Routine work.	
	5/5		General Routine work. Dump Stops etc.	

WAR DIARY
or
INTELLIGENCE SUMMARY

(Erase heading not required.)

Army Form C. 2118.

Place	Date	Hour	Summary of Events and Information	Remarks and references to Appendices
Headsville	6/5		14th P.9.R. had a Lewis gun destroyed by shell fire, wired to replace B1283. Visited 1 of Infy Bde.	
	7/5		General Praelie wrote a rather large number of rifles coming into shops lately mostly repairable.	
	8/5		Thuech Lord of Lear Bottom came up for 110 Yrs Ame who have had to enlarge their accomodation.	
	9/5		Visited all T.M.B.s in connection with howitzers they have none except an indifferent sighting one.	

Place	Date	Hour	Summary of Events and Information	Remarks and references to Appendices
Headsville	10/5		General routine work; Received the Lewis gun winch for on 7/5. Called to I.O.M. 10th Corps at WARLOY.	
	11/5		2 Coys 1 (Princess) moved to MARTINSART, remainder to follow for AVELUY WOOD and remainder of Skel held (Require (am withdrawn from such our of line; temporarily.	
	12/5		Series for the ordin large tool storerams allowed under OS 9/2374 34-7 8/5/16. Vide 109th Infy Bde	

WAR DIARY
or
INTELLIGENCE SUMMARY

Army. Form C. 2118.

Place	Date	Hour	Summary of Events and Information	Remarks and references to Appendices
Heachville	13/5		Received scheme of Reorganization of D.A.C. and B.A.C. being worked. The Div. Arty. to be re-organized into 3. 18 pr Batteries and 1 How. Batty of Six 18 prs and one Batty of 3. 18 pr Battery	
	14/5		The Div. Cavalry & Div Cyclists to be withdrawn from the Div. 16 pr Divisional Cav. Regt. and Corps Cyclist Regt formed. The weather has held until we have permission to rotate & planted its end of month.	
	15/6		General Routine above. The failure I find who were originally assembled for battles i.e. making up from old ones are too useful at modeling long ranges & ago have have to be able to make many fuller. There seem to be an increasing number of special odd things to be done through extension Trench Warfare	

249 Wt. W14957/M90 750,000 1/16 J.B.C. & A. Forms/C.2118/12.

WAR DIARY
or
INTELLIGENCE SUMMARY

Army Form C. 2118.

Place	Date	Hour	Summary of Events and Information	Remarks and references to Appendices
Houdeville	16/5		Wired for 20 Standard Horns & 90 Cylinders to complete to 35%	
	17/5	10.15.	Wired for Machine Gun to complete 6th Innis. Dragoons Service Squadron to two.	
	18/5		Wired 6th Innis. Dragoons to collect two Sacks Pack saddlery from O.O. 10th Corps Troops.	
	19/5		Wired for 57 magazines for Lewis Gun to replace defectives received	
	20/5		" " 24 " " " for 8th R.I.R. also wired 108th Bde. M.G. Coy. to send 16 w/s Mr. E. Bartels to Div. Armourers Shop Varennes.	
	21/5		General Routine Duties.	
	22/5		Purchased lantern for special road controls.	

WAR DIARY
or
INTELLIGENCE SUMMARY

Army Form C. 2118.

Place	Date	Hour	Summary of Events and Information	Remarks and references to Appendices
Hardinville	24/5		Hwd to Base for 55 magazines Lewis Gun to replace defectives for 15th R.I.R., also 39 for 13th R.I.R.	
	25/5		Hwd Base detailed changes of designations of our Artillery in accordance with their wire; also wired for 27 magazines Lewis Gun to replace defectives for 9th Skins.	
	26/5		Hwd Base for four magazines Lewis Gun to replace defectives: 10th Skins - 35 : 11th Skins - 28 : 9th R.I.F. - 40: 9th R.I.R. - 49: 12th R.I.R. 34.	
	27/5		Cable enquiry respecting rifles not yet up from Base.	
	28/5		Hwd Base for 26 magazines Lewis Gun to replace defectives for 16th R.I.R.	

Army Form C. 2118.

WAR DIARY
or
INTELLIGENCE SUMMARY

(Erase heading not required.)

Instructions regarding War Diaries and Intelligence Summaries are contained in F.S. Regs., Part II. and the Staff Manual respectively. Title Pages will be prepared in manuscript.

Place	Date	Hour	Summary of Events and Information	Remarks and references to Appendices
Headsville	29/5		D.R.O. 29/5 All ranks Blankets Mentl. Clo. incln. Boots Gum Thigh to be rtd. to Belle Eglise today	
	30/5		Commenced drawing stores from Achenne Railhead instead of Belle Eglise.	
	31/5		Wire from 247th (W.R.) Bde. F.A. enquiring if they may draw stores through us as they are attached to 10½ Corps Arty. Referred them to dadm 49th Div. 20,535. 2nd Blankets returned	
	1/6		"Have we any long bayonets for transfer" Wire from 49th Div. (Wired we can spare 15)	
	2/6		Saw A.D.O.S. about landing our cavalry to Corps.	
	3/6		Purchased special stove for Rain.	
	4/6		Visited units & office work.	

WAR DIARY
or
INTELLIGENCE SUMMARY
(Erase heading not required.)

Army Form C. 2118.

Place	Date	Hour	Summary of Events and Information	Remarks and references to Appendices
Meadwille	5/6		Wired G Corps that we handed over 1200 Blankets to H.H. C.E.S. today from Belle Eglise. (1) D.R.O. All Capts. N.P. to be reg'd B.A.D.O.S. on 6th inst. without fail. (2) D.R.O. Instruction concerning regulation of Stombos Horns.	
	6/6		Local purchase in AMIENS.	
	7/6	ang	Male arrangements to devoted underclothing before return to Base	
	8/6		D.R.O. Instructions as regards packing of o/s clothing retd.	
	9/6		No Hunter Clothing to be retd. to Paris until after 12th (Here 10th Corps.)	

Army Form C. 2118.

WAR DIARY
or
INTELLIGENCE SUMMARY
(Erase heading not required.)

Instructions regarding War Diaries and Intelligence Summaries are contained in F. S. Regs., Part II. and the Staff Manual respectively. Title Pages will be prepared in manuscript.

Place	Date	Hour	Summary of Events and Information	Remarks and references to Appendices
Hedauville	10/6		Made up special flags for G. Brennan in Tailors Shop.	
	11/6		Made arrangements for washing potrus Cans & re issuing for sundries Vends in trenches.	
	12/6		D.R.L.S. to Base. A/36 T.M.Bty. now attached to our Div.	
	13/6		D.R.O:- Time will be advanced 1 hour at 11 p.m. on the 14th inst.	
	14/6		Tents & Shelters delivered at Aveluy Wood for Y36 T.M. Bty. 10 of Skins & 25 Shelters left with R.E.	
	15/6		11th R.I.R. moved to Martinsart Wood.	

Army Form C. 2118.

WAR DIARY
or
INTELLIGENCE SUMMARY

(Erase heading not required.)

Instructions regarding War Diaries and Intelligence Summaries are contained in F. S. Regs., Part II. and the Staff Manual respectively. Title Pages will be prepared in manuscript.

Place	Date	Hour	Summary of Events and Information	Remarks and references to Appendices
Hedauville	14/6		MOVES:- 15th R.I.R. to Aveluy Wood: 1 Bn. 109th Bde. to Martinsart Wood. (14th R.I.R.?); 1 Bn. 109th Bde. to Aveluy Wood. (10th Skins?)	
	17/6		Arranged with Fourth Army Flying Squad. to have men taken for visiting "Panorama" for Signals to Aeroplanes.	
	19/6		D.R.O.:- Issue of Steel Helmets extended supply now as foll:- Infantry 75. (see D.R.O.) 4 Stokes Mortars issued to each Bde.	
	19/6		Read Lectures for the "Offensive"	
	20/6		Communication routes worn	

WAR DIARY
INTELLIGENCE SUMMARY

Army Form C. 2118.

Place	Date	Hour	Summary of Events and Information	Remarks and references to Appendices
Sedanville	21/6		Wire from I Corps :- Periscopes now available Havre, have we ordered?	
	22/6	14.25	Capt. H.P. returned to Base to date.	
	23/6		Rec'd Tents & Shelters from 108th Bde. Lancashire Dumps & 109th Bde. Martinsart Station Dump. Finished receiving Hunter Watching at Belle Eglise & brought marquees away after 2½ months.	
	24/6		Wired Base for 1 Vickers Gun .303 to replace for 109th Bde. M.G. Coy.	
	25/6		General routine work. Many urgent calls preparing to offensive.	
	26/6		Vickers Gun wired for 24th ulto: today. #3 Inniskilling Regt. wired 3 am. Wired for Lewis Gun .303 Lewis to draw from Railhead to replace for 15th R.I.R.	

Army Form C. 2118.

WAR DIARY
or
INTELLIGENCE SUMMARY
(Erase heading not required.)

Instructions regarding War Diaries and Intelligence Summaries are contained in F. S. Regs., Part II. and the Staff Manual respectively. Title Pages will be prepared in manuscript.

Place	Date	Hour	Summary of Events and Information	Remarks and references to Appendices
Ledeawille	27/6		<u>Move</u>. 1/3rd Monmouth Regt. to 49th Div. Wired for 2 Vickers Guns to replace u/s for 108th Bde. M.G. Coy.	
	28/6		Lewis Gun wired for 26th rec't. to-day. W.36 T.M. Bty. disbanded. Special Order of the Day by G.O.C. on coming offensive.	Wired 3.7.16 ... Bdos 26.7.16
	29/6		Wired for 166th Lewis Gun Carriers Magazine (Arty. D.O.S. OE 9816) Scale 16 per gun. Handed over outstanding stores & indents to D.A.D.O.S. Hq. Div. for 1/3" Monmouth Regt.	
	30/6		D.A.D.O.S. of Div. to may go to Corps Workshops for gun parts urgently required Arty. D.D.O.S. 4th Army. H.O. 59/1/3. X Corps #981/8. <u>Move</u>. Y 25 T.M. Bty. from 25th Div. to 36th Div.	

Army Form C. 2118.

WAR DIARY
or
INTELLIGENCE SUMMARY

(Erase heading not required.)

DADOS
36 DIV VOL 7
July 21/8.

Place	Date	Hour	Summary of Events and Information	Remarks and references to Appendices
Hedauville	1st	August?	The attack began at 7.30. Reports at 11 splendid. Demands for rifts supplied for securing prisoners to take up positions of necessary as far a possible on Ancicale.	
		2nd	Still moving on & no advance in ettio Huns let us have 1000 up employed so as to give all glass labels in exchange.	

Place	Date	Hour	Summary of Events and Information	Remarks and references to Appendices
Hebuterne	1st		Angres. The attack began at 7.30. Attack on L. Splendid advance to the objectives & seeing favour to the up return of Germany on two fronts on Amiens	
	2nd		Still holding on + no answer at all. Have 2d Aus line 150 & et empties so as to pour all Gds behind in reserve	

Army Form C. 2118.

WAR DIARY
or
INTELLIGENCE SUMMARY

(Erase heading not required.)

Instructions regarding War Diaries and Intelligence Summaries are contained in F. S. Regs., Part II. and the Staff Manual respectively. Title Pages will be prepared in manuscript.

Place	Date	Hour	Summary of Events and Information	Remarks and references to Appendices
Hedauville	3/7		5 Vickers Guns issued for 1st rei' to-day; from Abbeville. Issued for 4 Lewis Guns .303 to replace destroyed for 14th R.I.R.	
	4/7		Running out Springs Gun 15r - firing numerous trouble ?	
	5/7		4 Lewis Guns issued for 3rd rei' to-day. Issued position of Springs R.O. to I Corps.	
Rubempré	6/7		Move:- advised by o/c 36th Divnl. Arty. of the distribution of same:- 173 Bde. B'&'C'Bty: 15th Bde. } 153 Bde. } to 49th Division. on 5th. 172 " 246 " A'B 4' 154 Bde } to H9th Division on 5th. Divnl Hdqrs. left Hedauville for Rubempré. Instrs. from H.Q. that all demands on Base for Carriages, guns, Howitzers, machine guns & trench mortars to be repeated by wire to Q.M.G. GHQ.	

WAR DIARY or INTELLIGENCE SUMMARY

Army Form C. 2118.

Place	Date	Hour	Summary of Events and Information	Remarks and references to Appendices
Hédauville	3/7		5 Vickers Guns issued for 1st line to-day from Abbeville. Hurd for Lewis Guns 303 to replace destroyed for 1st R.I.R.	
	4/7		Transport of Spring O/B/SE/3 from town trucks	
	5/7		4 Lewis Guns issued for 3rd line to-day Hurd position of Spring R.O. to I Corps	
Rubempré	6/7		Move. Returned by O.C. 36th Divnl. Arty. of the distribution of amn:- 173 Bde. } to 149th Division on 5th B/C Bty. 15th Bde. } 12th Div: } 133 Bde 172 " 246 " "A" By. 154 Bde Reons Adjs. Capt. Hedowicke to Rubempré. Instr. from D.Q. that all ammonts on Bois for Carnoys guns Howitzers, Machine Guns & Trench mortars to be repeated by wire to O.H.G.H.Q.	

WAR DIARY
or
INTELLIGENCE SUMMARY

Army Form C. 2118.

Place	Date	Hour	Summary of Events and Information	Remarks and references to Appendices
Rubempré	7/7		Commenced drawing Stores from Vignacourt Railhead & issuing to Units from Lorries.	
	8/7		Immense quantities of all kinds of Stores received by units being unable to carry on first echelon transport owing to being able to carry on war establishment to B.E.F.	
	9/7		Handed over 800 odd Stall Kennels to 49th Division.	
	10/7		Left Rubempré (Somme) in evening & joined Supply Column at Mirvaux.	
	11/7		Ordnance Lorries travelled with Supply Col. & arrived Blaringhem 10 p.m., stayed night.	

WAR DIARY
or
INTELLIGENCE SUMMARY

Army Form C. 2118.

Place	Date	Hour	Summary of Events and Information	Remarks and references to Appendices
Rubempré	7/7		Commenced issuing Stores from Vignacourt Railhead. Issued Single items to all units.	
	8/7		Received quantities of all kinds of stores to be distributed by train from Vignacourt to units in the Divisional area (not much came through) & supplemented by lorries	
	9/7		Handed over 500 cwt Steel Helmets to 49th Division	
	10/7		Lieut Robinson (Somm?) is issuing & general Supply Officer is absence	
	11/7		Orders for the handled and Supply Col'n leave Rubempré 10pm. stops night ?	

Army Form C. 2118.

WAR DIARY
or
INTELLIGENCE SUMMARY
(Erase heading not required.)

Instructions regarding War Diaries and Intelligence Summaries are contained in F. S. Regs., Part II. and the Staff Manual respectively. Title Pages will be prepared in manuscript.

Place	Date	Hour	Summary of Events and Information	Remarks and references to Appendices
Silques	12/7		Divisional Headquarters at Silques from to-day.	
	13/7		Visited new Railhead at Watten. MOVES:- Hdqrs. & Batteries. 173 Bde. R.F.A. also B/154 & C/154 Brigade from 12th Div. to 36th Div.	
	14/7		Visited all Brigades at their new quarters. Issued Stores to all Units from Lorries, finished 11 p.m.	
	15/7		~~from~~ To-day, stores for all Units will be delivered to Bde. H.Q. MOVES. Y 25th T.M. Bty. from 36th Div. to 25th Div. (rec'd 17th): 153 Bde. R.F.A., A/154 Bty. R.F.A., 172 Bde. R.F.A. from 49th Div. to 36th Div. (rec'd 17th)	
	16/7		Reconnoying Smoke blends for reserve arrived at WATTEN railhead from Stores and handed thence to Save Cartage.	

Army Form C. 2118.

WAR DIARY
or
INTELLIGENCE SUMMARY

(Erase heading not required.)

Place	Date	Hour	Summary of Events and Information	Remarks and references to Appendices
Lizerne	12/7		Divisional Analysis at Lizerne from Entry	
	13/7		Various are Reinforced Battery Moves:- Hooper's Battery 173 Bde R.F.A. also B/154 & C/154 Brigade from 13th Div. to 36th Div.	
	14/7		Various all Brigades at same as before. Issued Orders to all units from Corps General 11 pm	
	15/7		5 way Scan for all units will to relieved to Bde H.Q. Moves Y.45 T.M. Bty. from 36th Div. to 25th Div. (no 17); 153 Bde R.F.A., A/154 Bty R.F.A., 173 Bde R.F.A. from 49th Div. to 36th Div. (no 17)	
	16/7		Reconnys enemy blush for waves ecenic at WATTEN railway from STO and hundred near to Serre Bridge	

WAR DIARY
or
INTELLIGENCE SUMMARY

Army Form C. 2118.

Place	Date	Hour	Summary of Events and Information	Remarks and references to Appendices
Tilques	17/7		Location of Units of Divnl. Artillery received. Accompanied J.O.M. to 3 Field Co. R.E. & inspected vehicles requiring repair. Condition under circumstances not bad.	
	18/7		At Calais, helper arranging spare hubs for F.T.E. whom I hear may leave soon. D.D.S. Second Army here.	
	19/7		Divnl. Artillery to I Corps. Workshop men from Calais at H.Q's R.E. Advised that we move to IV Corps.	
	20/7		103rd Bde. complained to Army they could not get stores, went into this & found to be no fault of ours, in fact H.Q. took stores for them when they refused them.	
	21/7		Divnl. Hqrs. left Tilques and opened at Enguelbeg.	

WAR DIARY or INTELLIGENCE SUMMARY

Army Form C. 2118.

Place	Date	Hour	Summary of Events and Information	Remarks and references to Appendices
Isques	17/7		Location of Units of Divnl. Artillery received. Accompanied I.O.A. to 3 Field Cos R.E. inspected wheels requiring repair. Considerable unevenness but not extensive.	
	18/7		At Calais where wagon spare parts for TTE return & have been seen. DDOS Seine & Army	
	19/7		none	
			Divnl. Artillery to I Corps Workshop men from Calais at H.Q.s R.E. Assured that we were to have IV Corps.	
		20/7	108" Bde. complained to Army they could not get stores, went into this & found to be no fault of ours, in fact W.O. took stores for them this day & they refused to accept them.	
	21/7		Divnl. Hdqrs. left Isques and opened at Coyecques	

WAR DIARY
or
INTELLIGENCE SUMMARY
(Erase heading not required.)

Army Form C. 2118.

Place	Date	Hour	Summary of Events and Information	Remarks and references to Appendices
Esquelbecq	22/7		Dump left Esquelbecq for Bailleul, railhead Steenwerck.	
	23/7		Work. Hdqrs left Esquelbecq for Mont Noir, this place is not convenient for us as regards Dump so we joined them at farm 1 Kilo outside Bailleul. We are now in V Corps & have our original Artillery again. 20th Div. D.A.D.O.S. who was on the farm left for the south. A.D.O.S. V Corps here. Position of Dump S.9.B.C. Sheet 28.	
Bailleul (farm)	24/7		Very busy day receiving, issuing and finding units.	
	25/7		Dump very convenient for stores but most inconvenient for roads. A.A.&Q.M.G. insists on moving dump to Sheet 36. B.1. Central. Ourselves very indifferent	

WAR DIARY
or
INTELLIGENCE SUMMARY

Army Form C. 2118.

Place	Date	Hour	Summary of Events and Information	Remarks and references to Appendices
Esquelbecq	22/7		Jump tpt Esquelbecq for Bailleul, reached Steenwerck.	
	23/7		Sent Major tpt Esquelbecq for transit Thou, the place is not convenient for us as regards dump as we joined them at farm 1 mile outside Bailleul. We are now in I Corps Area. Saw original Bailleul again. 2nd Div. DADOS who was in the farm tpt for the south. A.D.O.S. I Corps here. Postin 1 Div. S.9. O.S. Sh. 28.	
Bailleul	24/7		Very busy day receiving various cars future work	
	25/7		Damp. Very occupied for stores but not movement for north. AA&QMG wrote to A.A.G. M.G. (Gunston) for ... day to G.H.Q. 36. B. 1 suls.	

WAR DIARY
INTELLIGENCE SUMMARY

Place	Date	Hour	Summary of Events and Information	Remarks and references to Appendices
Bailleul	27/7		Very long parade of stores received owing to issue not being able to have a thorough overhaul since the Battle of July 1st and being (250) unequipped of Shell helmets drawn going well & still many things coming to arrive of leaving than very long, due to have to be overhauled which was secured last year too.	
	28/7		Sent in Chechies to new Dump with some stores. Hired Second Army that Bivort, Anti-Gas School is not yet in possession of Box Respirators & Spare Face Piece but have wired these today.	
	29/7		The office left Bailleul (Farm) for Sh 36 B f. 7. Kilemetre S.E from Bailleul. D.A.Q. remain at Monte Noir. Unit draw from new Dump. Cleared all Armourers material and sheds from Farm. A DOS I Corps at new Dump.	
	31/7		Many alterations & improvements to dump to carry out Railway in front of line a great source of trouble in providing & interfere greatly with this.	

Mincelay Capt
DOS 4

WAR DIARY
or
INTELLIGENCE SUMMARY
(Erase heading not required.)

Army Form C. 2118.

Place	Date	Hour	Summary of Events and Information	Remarks and references to Appendices
Bailleul	27/7		Very Long Visibility (Stereoscopic) survey to ascertain all entities to have the Stereoscope employed during the attack of July 31st and say (350) employed of that date	
	28/7		drew you will & still many things every two minutes at which however than very long, but to be watched & not too much crammed	
	29/7		Sent to Cheshire to new Dump will some stores. Hired Steam Lorry that does Argh Gas School in order to get an increase of Box Respirators. Some Face Pieces but have saved these today.	
	30/7		The three type Ballast (turn) for Bu 36, B51 allotted S.E. from Bailleul. R.H.Q. remain at Mont Noir. Unit draw from new Dump Clement all Armourers material and sheds from Farm. A DOS I Corps at new Dump.	
	31/7		Many alterations & improvements to Unit to Carry out today in hopes of being a great source of trouble in matters & protection quite by these	

(Illegible signature) Cpt Blanq

WAR DIARY
or
INTELLIGENCE SUMMARY of AA&QMG of 36th Div Vol 8

(Erase heading not required.)

Army Form C. 2118.

Place	Date	Hour	Summary of Events and Information	Remarks and references to Appendices
Ostes B. Central	1/8		8 Tons Stores arrived from Base. Getting straight in our new place.	
	2/8		All important Artillery Store received. A.D.O.S. V Corps here. A.A.Q.M.G. hen went through outstandings with him.	
	3/8		Visited Specialists School, Labour Battalion & Corps	
	4/8		Visited 2nd Army Headquarters at Cassel. Copy from "Q" of M.G.C's letter of 11/10/15 regarding Returns. "Units have not paid sufficient attention to replies & return of late"	
	5/8		Wire from Calais. 1000 Steel Helmets despatched for us to-night. V Corps. Position of Tentage. 18 Serviceable. 18 doubtful being sent to Base. Instructions from Corps to demand 18 to replace.	

WAR DIARY
or
INTELLIGENCE SUMMARY

Army Form C. 2118.

Place	Date	Hour	Summary of Events and Information	Remarks and references to Appendices
B1 Central	6/8		Bde. Major of 108th here, conversation regarding recent complaint of that Bde.	
	7/8		At Cassel. A.D.O.S. 5th Corps here. Made enquiries as to local purchase of mincing machines for own & 41st Div. Wire from 2nd Corps asking if two 18 pdr. guns no. H34H & 5147 are with us. Major R.A. wired that no. H34H is in A/154 & no. 5147 is not with us, repld. to 2nd Corps.	
	8/8		New purchaser in Hazebrouck and Office all afternoon & evening	
	9/8		Was very hot riding & cycling which takes up a great deal of time from department duties	

WAR DIARY
or
INTELLIGENCE SUMMARY

(Erase heading not required.)

Army Form C. 2118.

Place	Date	Hour	Summary of Events and Information	Remarks and references to Appendices
B/ Corbul	10/8		Advised A.Q, R.A. by wire of One 9.45 Trench Mortar available & asked them to arrange removal.	
	11/8		Had fatigue party of 25 men (R.E.'s) working on ridging D.O.S. Dpt Dump there with C.I.O.M. let fr... I went to Base (wire) for 25 Tank C.S.L. to replace repairable being sent. Tools accumulators for horses (as warning) to be recharged to D.R.C. and saw work.	
	12/8		No one in office though workers to see work in afternoon.	
	13/8		A.D.O.S. phoned about fortnightly M.G. return. We sent this to H.Q. yesterday being under the impression they sent copy to Corps. However sent copy to Corps by 8.30pm R.d.S.	

WAR DIARY
or
INTELLIGENCE SUMMARY

Army Form C. 2118.

Place	Date	Hour	Summary of Events and Information	Remarks and references to Appendices
B I Central	14/8		Moves. No. 2 Kite Balloon Sec. R.F.C. & No. 4 Siege Coy. R.M.R.E. from 36th Div. to 19th Div. Thence from IV Corps to IX Corps.	
	15/8		B/Genl. Dudley I Corps + Lt-Col Rouger IX Corps called.	
	16/8		Visited units called on A.D.O.S. IX Corps, having most unsatisfactory news I can to some days, it being stated to my use nominally but I receive intimations from "Q" to call & bring up different officers in send any stated hours to certain places, interfering with Departmental work.	
	17/8		Hear from "Q":- "Batn. report they have very few Dummy Cartridges. will we please indent for some." Hived Base B 1866 of 17/5/16.	

WAR DIARY
or
INTELLIGENCE SUMMARY

(Erase heading not required.)

Army Form C. 2118.

Place	Date	Hour	Summary of Events and Information	Remarks and references to Appendices
B1 Central	18/8		No car until 9 p.m. when I visited A.D.O.S. IX Corps.	
	19/8		Capt. Mackenzie went on leave.	
	20/8		Local Purchase in morning. Commenced construction of slipper road 15 metres standing for lorries in wm. lis. shelters from R.E.	
	21/8		To Hazebrouck for L.P. Visited R.E Workshops re armour' plates at Borre and Rifle Stands received from Salvage.	
	22/8		Visited A.D.O.S. IX Corps re tents & IX Corps Workshops.	
	23/8		To Hd. Qrs. 36th Divn. "Q" re maintenance spares.	

WAR DIARY
or
INTELLIGENCE SUMMARY

Army Form C. 2118.

Place	Date	Hour	Summary of Events and Information	Remarks and references to Appendices
B.1 Cav Fd	24/8		To Bailleul for Local Purchase. (Lorries for roads material renewed for making standing for transport drawing stores. Working party of 10 from APM to spread road material (for this any?)	
	25/8		Visited Special School of Instruction. Afterwards to Hazebrouck to purchase various stores from Div. Stn. Sd. of Instruction as ordered by "Q".	
	26/8		Called on A.D.O.S. IX Corps. IX Corps. Worsthof. with TM 117/1 re Sadles & 15 de new Brassards.	
	27/8		Capt. Mackenzie in return from leave	

WAR DIARY
or
INTELLIGENCE SUMMARY
(Erase heading not required.)

Army Form C. 2118.

Place	Date	Hour	Summary of Events and Information	Remarks and references to Appendices
B. Central	28/8		In morning in office afternoon called on A.D.O.S IX Corps & Div Hd. Qrs. & Q.F.M.	
	29/8		Went Local Purchasing in afternoon, bought Electric Torches for 109th Bde.	
	30/8		Emphasized to certain Arty. Units as they P.H. Helmets are not available they must draw "P.H." when they are short, and always have a stock "in" units at 108 Bde Hd Qrs & went into administration question	
	31/8		A.A. & Q.M.G. here in morning. Visited Batteries in line to inspect respirators shelling heavy. In afternoon called on A.D.O.S. IX Corps and several units	

Munsderie Captain
A.D.O.S.
36th

WAR DIARY *or* **INTELLIGENCE SUMMARY**

Army Form C. 2118.

DADOS 36th Division

Vol 9

Place	Date	Hour	Summary of Events and Information	Remarks and references to Appendices
B. 1. Central	1/9		Rec'd from Corps particulars of Scheme for equipping the Div. with Small Box Respirators & procedure to be taken. Divnl. Hdqrs. moved from Mont Noir to St. Jans Cappel. A'D'R' Cavalry Wing Parted again 1st Cav. Div. tomorrow.	
	2/9		Went to Calais with ADOS about several question arising within the District and find the position much clearer. Having found under for no. 7 Ord. Sqn. which were lying up, the orders which were not known [previous] to Calais had received further instructions which to do.	(30" Army troops from 34 & 31 Div. 1st & 2nd Army troops)
	3/9		Office in morning. AA & QMG here. Went to 109th Bde. HQ. picked up Capt. Moore & visited that Bde's proposed new quarters. Arranged for Bde. Ordnance H.O. & men to proceed with Brigade. Rationy/Barefoot Local Purchase in morning Hazebrouck, Bailleul, bought hinges for C.R.E. 109th Bde. move postponed until 6th inst.	poplin/G.S. Blanket for Winter 3000.
	4/9			
	5/9		Called at IX Corps workshops & ADOS of Corps who was laid up. Difficulty in finding a French machine gun influenced in order I can get one the same as we had in 4th Army. Artillery to be rearmed [...] with [...]	

WAR DIARY
or
INTELLIGENCE SUMMARY

(Erase heading not required.)

Army Form C. 2118.

Place	Date	Hour	Summary of Events and Information	Remarks and references to Appendices
B1 Central	6/9		109th Bde. W.O. & men opened store at Dranoutre, 1 lorry to be with them permanent. Went to Cassel, 2nd Army H.Qrs. in afternoon.	
	7/9		Went to Hazebrouck & R.E. Workshops with Staff Capt. & Machine Gun Officer of 108th Bde. to see about Machine Gun Mountings, French Rifle Bayt. & Pivot Mountings. These were supplied through Ordnance in 4th Army but come through R.E. in this Army.	
	8/9		Visited 109th Fd. Amb., Divnl. Baths, Divnl. Train & Dranoutre from where Stores are now being issued to 109th Bde.	
	9/9		4 truck loads of Stores from Base incln. 12 Lewis Gun Handcarts, 4000 Box Respirators Small & Book Gun Thigh.	
	10/9		In office in morning. Recd. phone message from A.D.O.S. to go & see him at once, obtained car after lunch & went to see him. He moved to be at A.D.O.S. office for a short time as Col. Brogden very ill.	

Army Form C. 2118.

WAR DIARY
or
INTELLIGENCE SUMMARY

(Erase heading not required.)

Instructions regarding War Diaries and Intelligence Summaries are contained in F. S. Regs., Part II. and the Staff Manual respectively. Title Pages will be prepared in manuscript.

Place	Date	Hour	Summary of Events and Information	Remarks and references to Appendices
B. Central	11/9		MOVE. 171st Tunnelling Coy. R.E. from 19th Division to 36th Div. also, 36th Divnl. Supply Col. from 9th Corps Troops to Ord. 36th Div.	
	12/9		Went to 2nd Army Hdqrs. at Cassel. Certified by 108th Bde. that they are complete with Steel Helmets to depôt for #5 for 9th Rye. Irish Fus².	
	13/9		Local Purchase to Dunkirk in morning. In office in afternoon. Big supply of 1st Blankets coming up for Winter. Also collected Boots Gum Thigh from IX Corps Troops.	
	14/9		Went to Hazebrouck in afternoon, visited units, 2nd Army Workshops & A.D.O.S.	
	15/9		In morning went to Eransente & A.D.O.S. & visited Units. To Hazebrouck in afternoon.	

Army Form C. 2118.

WAR DIARY
or
INTELLIGENCE SUMMARY

(Erase heading not required.)

Instructions regarding War Diaries and Intelligence Summaries are contained in F. S. Regs., Part II. and the Staff Manual respectively. Title Pages will be prepared in manuscript.

Place	Date	Hour	Summary of Events and Information	Remarks and references to Appendices
B. Outra.	16/9		Issuing 1008 prs Boots Gum Thigh to H.Q. 109th, 108th & 109th Inf. Bde. Recd. 1750 Steel Helmets to Base this surplus being accounted for by 9th Entrenchg. Bn. leaving Div. & reduction in strength of Artillery.	
	17/9		In office in morning. Went to 2nd Army H.Q. & A.D.O.S. Corps in afternoon. Recd. letter re reducing correspondence by D.R.L.S., wrote Corps that it will be very inconvenient for any DRs to be signed by me.	
	18/9		No Car. In office all day. 7000 more Small Box Respirators from Base.	
	19/9		Local Purchase at Hazebrouck. 109th Bde. H.Q. in evening with regard to Flapper Fans.	
	20/9		In office all day except for couple of hours in afternoon when I rod to Mob. Vet. & A.S.C. Corps Funded 56 Lewis Gun Handcarts from Base.	

2:49 Wt. W14957/M90 750,000 1/16 J.B.C. & A. Forms/C.2118/12.

WAR DIARY or INTELLIGENCE SUMMARY

Army Form C. 2118.

Place	Date	Hour	Summary of Events and Information	Remarks and references to Appendices
Bi Aubut	21/9		Rec'd all Tents not in use (about 50 up) & H3 unserviceable) to R'head for dispatch to Base, but rec'd phone message from Cap- saying they reg'd the new ones, was able to stop these & send 19".	
	22/9		S.W.O to draw them from R'head tomorrow. Artillery Stores rendered surplus thro' re-organisation of Arty. returned to Dump. Have complete list & will compare with outstanding indents before returning to Base.	
	23/9		No car exept for urgent call to Hazebrouck	
	24/9		No Car available. Have very enjoyable but too great a mail of time when away	

WAR DIARY
or
INTELLIGENCE SUMMARY

(Erase heading not required.)

Army Form C. 2118.

Place	Date	Hour	Summary of Events and Information	Remarks and references to Appendices
B1 Central	25/9		To the Caválair, unable to find Brocard or but Thompson, tried to get word in time nor spare in office. Reported to Army the situation of Small Box Respirators.	
	26/9		Went to Calais to see about several matters with Field Indents.	
	27/9		Remained at Calais all day in Receipts under instruction & for information re-returned Stores with A.D.O.S	
	28/9		Rec'd wire from my office stating requirements of 108th Bee. I purchased locally & arrived back at B1 Central 10.30 pm.	
	29/9		In office in morning attending to number of things which cropped up in my absence. Col Brogden here. Went to Steenwerck & met Bde Major of 108th Bde. Col Hall called at office whilst I was away.	

WAR DIARY
or
INTELLIGENCE SUMMARY

Army Form C. 2118.

Place	Date	Hour	Summary of Events and Information	Remarks and references to Appendices
B1 Central	30/9.		Nothing worthy of note. Staff P.O.L. & A.D.O.S. IX Corps. Are now available to keep.	

Munroeberie Capt.
D.A.A.G. 36 Div.

DADOS Vol 10
36th Division

Army Form C. 2118

WAR DIARY
or
INTELLIGENCE SUMMARY
(Erase heading not required.)

Instructions regarding War Diaries and Intelligence Summaries are contained in F.S. Regs., Part II and the Staff Manual respectively. Title Pages will be prepared in manuscript.

Place	Date	Hour	Summary of Events and Information	Remarks and references to Appendices
B¹ Central	1/10		In office most of day. Sent painter to 107th Bde. H.Q. to do urgent luminous painting on Trench Mortar.	
	2/10		Had car all day, went to Hazebrouck & Poperinghe in afternoon	
	3/10		Nothing very special in office most of day.	
	4/10		Visited with 109 Bde. 110th Field Amb. & Rest Station all in afternoon. In office all morning.	
	5/10		Spent most of day in car looking for travelling kitchen which has been lost by F.A., went as far as Liproe. Also visited School of Sniping & St. Omer.	

WAR DIARY
or
INTELLIGENCE SUMMARY

Army Form C. 2118.

Place	Date	Hour	Summary of Events and Information	Remarks and references to Appendices
B1 Central	6/10		In office in morning. Visited Dump at Branoutre in afternoon. Hastened return of Spare Stores to one or two units. Recd 4 Large Box Repeaters to Base.	
	7/10		Move No. 4 Siege Coy RE. Advised to be galvanised by Army distinctive indication. Had an all day I went to 2nd HQ at Hazebrouck & also to 9/172.	
			Hazebrouck. Move 529th How. Bty. RFA joined Div. Will be known as 9/172.	
	8/10		4 Truck loads of Stores from Base inclu. 91 bale winter clothing Vests & Drawers Woollen. In office most of day, out after tea.	
	9/10		Visited D Corps concerning weakness of types for T.Ms. I.O.M. will make alteration by putting hard wood blocks in tubes. Went to Army H.Q. 109th Bde & visited units.	
	10/10		Went to 108th Bde. H.Q., 169th Bde. Div. H.Q. & L.P. in morning.	
	11/10		Visited 107th Infy Bde & dump, Army Workshop at Hazebrouck and 107th Infy Bde Hd Qrs. Received 10000 of the 30000 Cafes mandrils for the Des plungers not to be replaced when worn out.	

2449 Wt. W14957/M90 750,000 1/16 J.B.C. & A. Forms/C.2118/12.

WAR DIARY
or
INTELLIGENCE SUMMARY

(Erase heading not required.)

Army Form C. 2118.

Place	Date	Hour	Summary of Events and Information	Remarks and references to Appendices
B.I. Central	12/10		Received instructions to return to Base all our reserve of P.H. Helmets that are being small "Three Nut" kind for storage of Box Respirators.	
	13/10		Visiting units & general departmental work. Received 3000 more cases. Rec'd official notification of arrival of 529 Ham. Bty. mechanics.	
	14/10		Visits units of 106 Siege Bty, Devonshires & 109th Bde, & Ad Qrs Decodes to have new hut building for office & petitioned accordingly. Present office very cold will be used for storage of Reserves.	
	15/10		In office all morning. Two Armrs from 1st Australian Div M.G. Coy have 6 days instructional in Lens Auth: Shop. Reported to A.D.O.S. 1st Anzac.	
	16/10		In office all morning. In afternoon at Second Army Workshops.	
	17/10		Visits units 109th & 110th Bdes & Hd Qrs, & also went over to Second Army about various small details of departmental work.	

WAR DIARY
or
INTELLIGENCE SUMMARY

Army Form C. 2118.

Place	Date	Hour	Summary of Events and Information	Remarks and references to Appendices
B1 Central	18/10		Made arrangements for letters in these Divisions & k higher to be sent for onward despatch with transpt.	
	19/10		Visited Bangalore Arty Gas school & Div Hd Qrs.	
	20/10		Returned call about 2.15 started when Hd Qrs informed me could now be trans'd to Wire from Base. "No stores to-night"	
	21/10		Greek Funerary in Wareham & to 2nd Army Workshop with Sen M.G. Officers about trench mountings ex. Means not received as an Hd free. ubicetine hut no stores.	
	22/10		2 days Stores from Base, Service Dress & Camp Equipment also 2650 Blankets. Rather quiet day.	
	23/10		Attended conference at 107th Bde H.Q. 10 am. Loaned 10 Primus Stoves to 107th & 108th Bdl. H.Q.	

Army Form C. 2118.

WAR DIARY
or
INTELLIGENCE SUMMARY

(Erase heading not required.)

Instructions regarding War Diaries and Intelligence Summaries are contained in F. S. Regs., Part II. and the Staff Manual respectively. Title Pages will be prepared in manuscript.

Place	Date	Hour	Summary of Events and Information	Remarks and references to Appendices
B/Cadre	24/10		8 Truck loads of Stores from Base inclu. 3500 Horse Rugs & 11,000 Drawers Woollen. Re: information that T.M. 9.45's are not to be demanded from Base at present as G.H.Q. are regulating distribution.	
	25/10		Office work & base purchase. Received note from Corps from G.H.Q. on re-equipping Divisions withdrawn from the line.	
	26/10		Had two officers from Calais, conversation on various departmental items. Diaries 109th Bde.	
	27/10		Went to Hazebrouck in afternoon & H.Q. in morning.	
	28/10		Office work. Reviews haw on "Horse Rugs".	
	29/10		Went to Calais for day to settle various Departmental matters.	
	30/10		Conference at 109th Infy Bde HQ of all Staff Captains & AA+QMG. Visited units. Wools Clothing from Base includes 5000 Vests & 9300 Drawers Woollen. Contracted influenza & advised by Doc. stay in bed a day or two.	
	31/10		109 Bde in morning. Contracted influenza & advised by Doc. stay in bed a day or two.	

Army Form C. 2118.

WAR DIARY
or
INTELLIGENCE SUMMARY
(Erase heading not required.)

DADOS 36th Div. Vol XI

Place	Date	Hour	Summary of Events and Information	Remarks and references to Appendices
B/ Central (Re Seule)	1/11 to 7/11		—	
	8/11		Capt. Mackenzie returned from Rest Station.	
	9/11		Visited units and 109 & 108 Hd Qrs. Also at Haybrook 15 Army workshops & local funerals.	
	10/11		Office work all day except to A.D.O.S. in evening.	
	11/11		Office	
	12/11		Went to H.Q. & Corps in morning in connection with clock of Bosh Gun Thigh. No Buck stores arrived from Base.	
	13/11		Went to 107th Bde conference with Col. Comyn in morning. Two days Buck stores from Base. Pickering Gear & necessaries officers were in afternoon.	

WAR DIARY
or
INTELLIGENCE SUMMARY

(Erase heading not required.)

Army Form C. 2118.

Place	Date	Hour	Summary of Events and Information	Remarks and references to Appendices
B.I Central	14/11		In office all day, no car, Heard that 2 3" Stokes Mortars are being sent up from Calais for instructional purposes.	
	15/11		MOVE 3rd Canadian Tunnelling Coy. C.E. from Ord. 9th Corps Troops to Ord. 36th Division. A.D.O.S. here in morning. No car so walked.	
	16/11		To 107th Bn. H.Q. in morning & local purchase at Hazebrouck in afternoon. Also took Stokes Tf. Cylinder to be filled at Army Workshops.	
	17/11		Pulled Rifles Qn. 1 of Infy. Bde. 1300 fm. Cards were arrived.	
	18/11		Pulled "108 Infy. Bde. 600 Gum Boot Finishes allotted to this Bn. and drawn. A.A. & Q.M.G. here in morning. A.D.O.S. in afternoon. Made further issue of Gum Boots Thigh as per "Q" distribution.	
	19/11		In office all day, no car, Issued Leather Jerkin to Trench Mortar Bty. & Machine Gun Coy.	
	20/11		107th Bn. Conference in morning. Office in afternoon & Called at A.D.O.S. in evening.	

WAR DIARY
or
INTELLIGENCE SUMMARY

(Erase heading not required.)

Army Form C. 2118.

Place	Date	Hour	Summary of Events and Information	Remarks and references to Appendices
B1 Central	22/11		In office in morning. Walked to Balleul & back in afternoon. Drew 3 special Mess Tins. M.S. from Corps (things on outside) & issued to D.A.D.T.C. for repair.	
	23/11		Visited Corps & 109th Bn. in morning. Hazebrouck in afternoon.	
	24/11		In office all morning, afternoon visited arrivals & base present. 15 lanterns for Amm. Dumps when Qurtraken. Called on A.D.O.S. 9. 10q Bde in morning. Walked to Sw trenches in afternoon.	
	25/11		7 tons of Stores from Base including 30 Soyer Stoves & 24 Lewis Machine Guns, these complete Bns. to 10 guns. In office in morning. To Div. H.Q. in afternoon & A.D.O.S.	
	26/11		To Div. H.Q. in morning & had interview with General Nugent. Ryan from A.O.S. through Div. Q. to explain abnormal issue of Gaiters for Aug (2335). It appeared to be a 5 week month & Artillery had just returned to div.	
	27/11		A.D.O.S. here in morning, discussed various departmental matters & explained system. To Hazebrouck in afternoon, local purchase. New man arrived Pte Cook in place of Pte Mills, evacuated sick.	

Army Form C. 2118.

WAR DIARY
or
INTELLIGENCE SUMMARY

(Erase heading not required.)

Instructions regarding War Diaries and Intelligence Summaries are contained in F. S. Regs., Part II. and the Staff Manual respectively. Title Pages will be prepared in manuscript.

Place	Date	Hour	Summary of Events and Information	Remarks and references to Appendices
St Aubin	28/11		In office in morning. A.D.O.S. called & went with him to visit Avril Bath, H.Q. 107 Bde.	
	29/11		Local Purchase in morning.	
	30/11		Visited units in morning & went to Calais after lunch.	

Mackenzie Capt
D.A.D.O.S. 36 Div.

WAR DIARY or INTELLIGENCE SUMMARY

Army Form C. 2118.

D.A.D.O.S
36th Division
Vol 12

Place	Date	Hour	Summary of Events and Information	Remarks and references to Appendices
B. Cutrul	1/12		At Calais all day settling various departmental matters. Issued balance of Capes Mackintosh to H.Q. R.A.[210] H.Q. R.E.[2] & 16 R.I.R.[30]	
	2/12		No stores up until noon. 50 Lamps R.R.T.P. from Base. No-one all day, usual departmental routine. Impressed upon certain units the necessity for keeping demand of Pantaloons — Bags More as low as poss. Train with stores late still to-day. Stores not ready for issue until 3.30 pm when majority of units had gone. Office again all day.	
	3/12			
	4/12		At D.H. Q. in morning & to Hazebrouck in afternoon trying to get batteries to fetch which are urgently reqd. & use niting avoiding H/B Base.	
	5/12		33 Hot Food Containers arrived from Base asked "Q" for cloths to Hazebrouck in afternoon, found rifles for Torch @ 15 e.a. would take two for a Torch & small Torch 3½/- complete informed H.Q. R.A.	
	6/12		Salvage Dump moved to field opposite our Ordnance Dump which makes matters much more convenient as regards return of stores to Base.	
	7/12		In office all morning & put everything straight. Capt. Mackenzie went on leave 3 p.m. Rec'd quotab. for Slot Board Containers:- 3rd 107/108; B'lis 4 each; HQ 109 B'lis -16; 16th R.I.R - 9	

Army Form C. 2118.

WAR DIARY
or
INTELLIGENCE SUMMARY
(Erase heading not required.)

Instructions regarding War Diaries and Intelligence Summaries are contained in F. S. Regs., Part II. and the Staff Manual respectively. Title Pages will be prepared in manuscript.

Place	Date	Hour	Summary of Events and Information	Remarks and references to Appendices
St Omer	8/12		Lt Cheetor will be acting D.A.D.O.S while Capt. Mackenzie is on leave.	
	9/12		Accompanied A.D.O.S IX Corps on a visit to Advance Dump at Arneke, Salvage dump at 109 & 104 Brigade Adv dump at De Seule — at Dranoutre A.O.D arrived for attachment for instruction.	
		10.—	Visited Advance Dump at Dranoutre.	
		11.—	Went to Hazebrouck to Heavy Mobile workshops 2nd Army on question of Cylinders. (Ordnance Artizans)	
		12.—	Nil	
		13.—	Went to Bailleul, Hazebrouck, St Omer & Calais Ancillary Workshops	

WAR DIARY
or
INTELLIGENCE SUMMARY

(Erase heading not required.)

Army Form C. 2118.

Place	Date	Hour	Summary of Events and Information	Remarks and references to Appendices
Bt Central	14/12		Coal Routine, made inspection of Stores, & dump at Dranoute	
	15/12		Coal Routine.	
	16/12		Coal Routine.	
	17/12		Lt Humphries went to Corps Conference. A Dot rented Dumps also D.A.D.S. visited A.S.C. near Bt Ashebrowne & Ameline Nois.	
	18/12		General Cammodin visited Office Stores & Dumps.	
	19/12		Coal Routine. Wire received Capt Mackenzie granted 21 days sick leave by Medical Authorities in Rouen. A Sot visited	
	20/12		Coal Routine	
	21/12		Coal Routine	

WAR DIARY or INTELLIGENCE SUMMARY

Army Form C. 2118.

Place	Date	Hour	Summary of Events and Information	Remarks and references to Appendices
At Rubad	22/12		A.D.O.S. visited dumps & Coffee — Usual routine —	
	23/12		Usual routine	
	24/12		Usual routine. New Armour Body Shields & Sick Nickleb arrived, first issue of 200 of each. 65 to each Bde. & 5 to Specialists Sect.	
	25/12		Closed down from 1 p.m. Det. had usual Xmas dinner. Smoke — the even'g —	
	26/12		A.D.O.S. visited — usual work. K. Ra Battery reference newest —	
	27/12		Purchased Clippers for Div Artillery & obtained some Lt. Hampshire Capt. to take up duties of A/D. DOS 25th Divn of Phosphor to take the D. DOS met a boat — usual routine	A.D.D.O.S. 36 Div.
	28/12		Usual routine.	
	29/12		Usual routine.	
	30/12		A.D.O.S visited Vert K Hafebbaneh, Amchur Stn, usual routine. Had ten cylinders Staghton Bomm filled at Shaykhpuek, delivered by Conv. Quarterly Return of Buck Lewis Guns Arrived to Specialists Sect.	
	31/12		Issues taken & A.D.O.S. No Car, fairly quiet day.	

WAR DIARY or INTELLIGENCE SUMMARY

Army Form C. 2118.

MGC Vol #5/3 36th Div

Place	Date	Hour	Summary of Events and Information	Remarks and references to Appendices
B. Central	1/1/17		24 Lewis Guns arrived from Base to complete Infty. Bns. to 12 guns. New programme of Bulk demands commenced. Obtained total Guns 1 boards required by A.O.S. & informed him.	
	2/1/17		10 Chaff-Cutting Machines arrived from Base, also 600 carriage Box Respirators to replace those issued previous to 21/9/16. A.O.S. here in morning. Went to Calais to settle one or two important matters. I purchased rifle for Jordan.	
	3/1/17		usual routine	
	4/1		usual routine	
	5/1		11 tons Stores from Base today being first of new arrangement whereby others only arrive every other day.	
	6/1		usual routine — a lot wanted, hope times or Haslemere	

WAR DIARY
or
INTELLIGENCE SUMMARY
(Erase heading not required.)

Army Form C. 2118.

Place	Date	Hour	Summary of Events and Information	Remarks and references to Appendices
B1 Central	7/1/17		9 Tons General Stores from Base.	
	8/1/17		Capt. Mackenzie returned from leave.	
	9/1/17		Returned from leave to duty yesterday when a word handed me by everybody in a word on record that his work in the Department and was glad to please to please on record that his work in the Department and was glad to please an officer for an officer for an officer most efficient for his months comfort and cleanliness and has been much improved for the months comfort and cleanliness and many improvements and the work running smoothly with no general convenience, and the work running smoothly with no complaint.	
	10/1/17		No cars in office all day	
	11/1/17		At about 3.30 P.M went to Army to see D.D.O.S. re Ord Cheques + in reference also took sample of new baking bag.	

Army Form C. 2118.

WAR DIARY
or
INTELLIGENCE SUMMARY

(Erase heading not required.)

Place	Date	Hour	Summary of Events and Information	Remarks and references to Appendices
B. Central	13/1		Local purchase in morning afternoon surveyed to see Bir Bakus.	
	14/1		Office work. No 7361 e/Sergt. (A/c) Brown arrived from I Corps for duty in preparation to fill vacancy of Condr. Chedere R.O.C. who will proceed to Calais.	
	15/1		Office work.	
	16/1		Office work & visiting hem huts.	
	17/1		Car for half-day. Chittle 107. Bde Comp. a/c Gunsmiths this unit of 108 Bde.	
	18/1		Office s. in afternoon to Second Army workshops & saw purchase of matinees for 8 utile travels for snow patrolling.	
	19/1		Further 25 Hot. food containers from Base making 58 received to date. Local purchase in morning, endeavouring to get Bleu Lamps for Arty. Also tried DAE for Soya Stoves for A.D.V.S.	

WAR DIARY
or
INTELLIGENCE SUMMARY
(Erase heading not required.)

Army Form C. 2118.

Instructions regarding War Diaries and Intelligence Summaries are contained in F. S. Regs., Part II. and the Staff Manual respectively. Title Pages will be prepared in manuscript.

Place	Date	Hour	Summary of Events and Information	Remarks and references to Appendices
De Scal.	20/1		Leave pursues for two ADV2. Officers leave completed, reserves for horse shortage & dumper etc. arranged.	
	21/1		Visited units & office work.	
	22/1		Visited units of 105 Infy Bde & ADV O.S. Drew 1000 francs for Cashier in office in afternoon.	
	23/1		Morning visited all Q.H.S. Stores of 107 Infy Bde at Branches. Called on A.D.O.S. and visited Q.M.S. of Branch In. & Trans In.	
	24/1		Visited units of 108 Infy Bde and 107 Infy Bde inspecting Q.M's stores. Re return of Bde Reinforcements issued prior to 21/1/17.	
	25/1		Visited A/15 D/173 B/15 & 4/17 as reserve of Bn Reinforcements, Q.M.G. evidently anxious, have handed all units. But refitting & intending in gen. shown there some.	
	26/1		Visited 108 Infy Bde re return of Bn Reinforcements. these previous. Had all from ADOS in afternoon.	
	27/1		Letter from "G" that all Bn Reps. have to be examined twice daily during frost. It is found that rubber tubes must carrying water to Valvis of firm & obtained & during afp cering burst Elfycering arrived back midnight.	

2449 Wt. W14957/Mg0 750,000 1/16 J.B.C. & A. Forms/C.2118/12.

Army Form C. 2118.

WAR DIARY
or
INTELLIGENCE SUMMARY
(Erase heading not required.)

Place	Date	Hour	Summary of Events and Information	Remarks and references to Appendices
Le Seut	28/1		Busy in office all morning. To 2nd Army H.Q. in afternoon.	London 25
	29/1		Got Ford Containers from Bone, making 83 to-date.	
	30/1		Office work in day. Nothing unusual to report.	
	31/1		Ind. Purchase sent to 2nd Army Workshops & Henry Mule. Rifle Bore Muslin running very low. Have received letter 9.0.H. 1X Corps unable to help with more Rifle B.M. Supplies to — Sent Arm. Staff Sergt. to Corps to obtain info on Bore. A.D.O.S. 1X Corps & S.O. Mecum A.O.D. Field the Dump were there at once.	

Wheesley
Capt.
D.A.D.O.S.
36th Division

WAR DIARY or **INTELLIGENCE SUMMARY**

Army Form C. 2118.

D.A.D.O.S. 36th Division

Place	Date	Hour	Summary of Events and Information	Remarks and references to Appendices
De Seule	1/2		No Car. Office work in morning. Worked to one or two neighbouring units in afternoon.	
	2/2		Office in morning & worked all afternoon to write hastening return of old Box Respirators to hurry receipts up to issues as soon as poss. to A.D.O.S.	
	3/2		Orders from "Q" had all fatigue men & Arm'r Acetal. medically examined & men return to their units tonight. Arm'r Sentcliffe (10" R.I.R.) & Arm'r Engelback (10" Skins) reported for duty in Arm'rs Shop.	
	4/2		In office again all day. Arm'r Ruling (12" R.I.R) & Arm'r Lynch (1" R.I.R) reported for duty in Div'nl. Shop making total of 6 Arm'r now employed.	
	5/2		Further 200 Armour Body Shield Steel Nickels from Base to Hazebrouck Bailleul. L.P. Shad Cylinder filled at Army Workshops. On going into question of excessive Nose Bags issued on complaint of R.A.M.C. it is found that for that quart'r (Oct/Nov/Dec) the average left of a Nose Bag was 6 to 7 weeks.	
	6/2		Office in morning Visiting Unit D.Q.F.T.Bn. in afternoon.	

WAR DIARY
or
INTELLIGENCE SUMMARY

Army Form C. 2118.

(Erase heading not required.)

Instructions regarding War Diaries and Intelligence Summaries are contained in F. S. Regs., Part II. and the Staff Manual respectively. Title Pages will be prepared in manuscript.

Place	Date	Hour	Summary of Events and Information	Remarks and references to Appendices
De Seule	7/2		Office in morning. Conference at Offices of ADOS IX Corps in afternoon. No O.C.'s forwards came up as small amount of material sent here are welcome remainder. This is not my arrangement & necessary steps being taken to prevent its continued. Cold extremely trying on saddle. Blankets horse rugs etc. many units having them lately some due they say to horses eating and often for "belley fits". Our painstaking and questioning afterwards is the result of the horses is unfit examination.	
	8/2		Office work. Still no component. Lewis gun at 15 x 24 Lewis Guns complete with spare parts arrived from Base completing Inf. Bns. to 14 guns each. No Bays Mire from Base this week.	
	9/2		Went to Calais after lunch & finding it late when finishing work remained the night. Went particularly to see about Breech Mechanisms.	
	10/2		Ret'd from Calais at mid-day. Office all afternoon & night. 60 South Canvas clothing up for men engaged in stripping horses for prevention of mange.	
	11/2		Office in morning. In afternoon to Hazebrouck to arrange material for local manufacture of slings for life firing of Lewis guns & No. 2 Army Workshops for oil bottles & repair of Browning frame.	
	12/2			

WAR DIARY or INTELLIGENCE SUMMARY

Army Form C. 2118.

Place	Date	Hour	Summary of Events and Information	Remarks and references to Appendices
Le Seule	13/2	10.30 am	Staff Captain: conference at English Farm field comp. A.T.Q.M.G. presiding. S.S.O. Sub Area Officer, Staff Captain & self present. I feel confident this meeting has saved me much writing.	
	14/2		Nothing much on to 2nd Army Workshops.	
	15/2		Visited unit of 10/15 with C.R.E. Item was turned on C.R.E. had to go to Ordnance Dump, which still has not arrived my own car to Ordnance Dump.	
	16/2		Visiting units the Mors. Equipments in afternoon and Loco Puiseux of Bois Poussenet.	
	17/2		Thaw restrictions to be imposed. No truck of Ordnance Stores due today.	
	18/2		4 ton General Stores from Base, truck brought down to R.E. Siding & then diverted to store dock, where it was unloaded under an hour.	
	19/2		No car, office all day, expecting A.D.O.S. who, however did not arrive.	
	20/2		Car arranged for at 11 A.M. arrived late & had to pick up C.R.E.	

WAR DIARY
or
INTELLIGENCE SUMMARY

(Erase heading not required.)

Army Form C. 2118.

Place	Date	Hour	Summary of Events and Information	Remarks and references to Appendices
The Seule	20/2		At 3. P.M. I arrived at 2nd Army Heavy Mortar during heavy driving rain in time to eat important business to be done in time (also lunch).	
	21/2		Visited A.D.O.S. IX Corps re the difficulty of the J.O.M. mortar & small items which are beyond the scope of wheelers & blacksmith owing to lack of tools for threading screws for nuts. The train wheelers & Smiths kept very busy going that would be condemned as the J.O.M. would not be able to do them for lack of time. If the J.O.M. cannot make there few things I am afraid many more weapons will be condemned.	
			Purchase lamps electric torch and dry battery. Supplies for helio demand & Artillery urgently hastening. The organisation of Bde. only now taking place & moves definitely made.	
	22/2			
	23/2		Have 113 Brigade Army Field Artillery now attached to this Division but received notification in evening that this Bde. will be attached to IX Corps Troops for Ordnance office all day. Reported to Div. H.Q. that the practice of the truck coming to be send during the week worked excellently & asking if arrangement could be made to continue the method	

Army Form C. 2118.

WAR DIARY
or
INTELLIGENCE SUMMARY

(Erase heading not required.)

Instructions regarding War Diaries and Intelligence Summaries are contained in F. S. Regs., Part II. and the Staff Manual respectively. Title Pages will be prepared in manuscript.

Place	Date	Hour	Summary of Events and Information	Remarks and references to Appendices
20 Seule	24/2		Car in afternoon, exchanged Bde. W.O. of 109" Bde. with W.O. of 107 Bde. at Dranoutre. Handed our stores & all outstandings of 113 Bde. R.F.A. to IX Corps Troops. Drew 1000 Cape Mac. from them.	
	25/2 Sun.		An exceptionally heavy day in the Office	
	26/2 Mon.		D.D.O.S. 2nd Army called in afternoon, I was out but met him on the road. He wished to know the present system of salvage. I explained I suggested a much better method would be to attack an exchanged Ord. Offr. by the Salvage Officer, he could Reg: rec'd of things coming in: also pick rated on nightly by A.O.O.	
	27/2 Tues.		Car from lunch time. To Hazebrouck and Ing. Supply Rdv.	
	28/2 Wed.		Visits with Div Artly Hd. Qrs. ADOS IX Corps, F.G.E. & Met new C.O	

Wheatherby Capt
DADOS 36th Division

WAR DIARY
or
INTELLIGENCE SUMMARY

Army Form C. 2118.

DADOS
36th Div.
Vol 15

Place	Date	Hour	Summary of Events and Information	Remarks and references to Appendices
Po Perle	1/3	THUR	Went to Calais at 3-30 with Slalis of Horse Clipping Machine. Artillery require these urgent on account of mange. To Sport 2nd Army of Timber issued since Jan. 1st.	to be Return
	2/3	FRI.	Saw D.O.S. while at Calais and D.D.O.S. L.of C. (N). Had a talk over Salvage & means of preventing waste. He was very keen on D.O.O. visits with an odd Spare hour & was of the opinion that in practice every Dir. these are visits too D.O.O.	
	3/3	SAT	MOVE:— 3rd Canadian Tunnelling Coy from 36th Division to II Anzac C.T. Very busy day. No Car.	
	4/3	SUN	Visited 109 Infy Bde & D.D.O.S. II Army. Brought from Army Trrorp O.O. a light Germann M.G. which was issued to 109 M.G. Coy.	
	5/3	MON	No Car today. walked in the afternoon.	
	6/3	TUES	No Car. Walked visiting units A.D.O.S. 4 Train and 109 Bde Hd Qrs.	
	7/3		General Detachment work	
	8/3		Much paperwork	

WAR DIARY
or
INTELLIGENCE SUMMARY

Army Form C. 2118.

Place	Date	Hour	Summary of Events and Information	Remarks and references to Appendices
Re Seule	9/3		Preliminary enquiries made	
	10/3		Told of Nov. of Div. to Dranoutre area & move of Ortreau at ADOS office worth Salvage. Suggested main salvage dump at Railheads to allow salvage by doing lightweight work. Removed all Isent. Boards to Dranoutre. Visited this place in afternoon when it is proposed my office should be but as the place is shelled regularly I suggested that we should go back to their farm which is close to Brilline Pres.	
	11/3		The 262 Rys. Construction Coy have arrived in Dranoutre area, will be accommodated by no for Ord. Visited Div. D.Q. & had conversation with A.A. & Q.M.G. with regard to move.	
	12/3		109 Bde. w.o. moved from Dranoutre to Fletre also 108 Bde. w.o. to Flêtre from De Seule. 107 Bde. w.o. took over at Dranoutre again. Nothing decided yet as to where my office shall be.	
	13/3		H.Q. of Divisional moves to Hille farm Sheet 28. S.9. 6. Rutrat or Mt. 19th. All the artillery enter H.Q. or 2 + 3 Section An. Col. drew from Dranoutre all the coys. 107 Inft Bde. T.M. Bs. So country S/Cart. Prevence & drink water from 109 Bde.	
	14/3			
	15/3		Visited Dranoutre & about & enter with him about arrangement	

WAR DIARY or INTELLIGENCE SUMMARY

Army Form C. 2118.

Place	Date	Hour	Summary of Events and Information	Remarks and references to Appendices
De Seule	16/3	Fri.	Visiting men	
	17/3	Sat.	Visited 107 Infty Bde Hd Qrs at Kemmel	
	18/3	Sun.	Lorries busy all day removing Reserve Store (Blankets, Repn. etc) to Dickie Farm. Sent one of my men to take over from unit going out.	
Dickie Farm	19/3	Mon.	Office moved to Dickie Farm from De Seule after being 7 months & 2 weeks at latter place.	
Sheet 28 S.9 Bcentral	20/3	Tues.	109 Infty Bde. learnt were training in Second Army Training Area were W Owen 16th Infty Bde moved up to trenches to forward area. 109 Infty Bde Dumping of Milk Gum boots & fuel etc. Collected from Stores Store at 10 p.m. Gum boots & delivd to 11th & 12th R.I.R finished at 1 A.M. No one expecting them QM had not been forwd	
	21/3	1 A.M.	& got up	

Place	Date	Hour	Summary of Events and Information	Remarks and references to Appendices
White Farm Shwebo S.9.B Cen.	21/3		Party arriving by Stony demonstration for presence of 109 Inf. Bde who are only to have improvised shelters which away. A.D.O.S. came round this afternoon & found all satisfactory.	
	22/3		Collected 12 lorry loads from Mktms dumps found by 109 Inf Bde Also issued out to Divisions & Units units of 10 7 Infty Bde. to B swills to 108 HQ Ors. 100 Tent from Base (the first of 300 advised by Army); received clothing from "Q" for 160 ors – 80 to 9 Ap Inni Fus & 80 to 13" R.I.R. also 7 tons General Store. very busy day.	
	23/3		Visited armourers & A.D.O.S. 1X Corps to salvage out.	
	24/3			
	25/3		Issues to 108 Bde & to Units 109" Offrs wear	
	26/3		Receiving urgent wires from 109 Bde Unit to indents, so that we can change the making provision but would like to know whether items of hum equipment to keep the batmans stores	

Army Form C. 2118.

WAR DIARY
or
INTELLIGENCE SUMMARY

(Erase heading not required.)

Instructions regarding War Diaries and Intelligence Summaries are contained in F. S. Regs., Part II. and the Staff Manual respectively. Title Pages will be prepared in manuscript.

Place	Date	Hour	Summary of Events and Information	Remarks and references to Appendices
	27/3/17		Went to Celers & brought away sufficient Finisby for the wants of 10 & Bee & believed in Bourtelegin.	
	28/3/17		Had Coln over ordnance walker & receiving demands by units of Chilling with the M.A. & Q.M.G. I consider it mainly due to the desire for suavenirs, and its only real check is to have sufficient salvage men so that they can all receipts & give a receipt, & I should only issue on being shown the receipt for previous issue of replacement.	
Hiera Farm	29/3		Rec'd list back from Salvage showing approximate receipts of Colo. Boots for week compared with my Bulk Issues of new stores. Sent Div. H.Q.	
"	30/3		Col. Comyn here in morning. Above Salvage figures not rec'd. I cannot be traced am preparing another immediately. Col. Comyn will arrange for a clerk for me to check carefully all Salvage receipts in accordance with suggestion about (28th) to 30 days 24 Lewis Guns from Base completes Div. to 16 guns per Battalion.	
"	31/3		Quarterly return sent in. Shows a substantial reduction in Q.D. & Boots. The Corp is instead W.A.M. 4451/A100/700/400 Wyel Ltd C.&Ap Forms/C.2118/12. but will have a lot of Winterings so. Capt. D. [signature] D.I.V.	

WAR DIARY
or
INTELLIGENCE SUMMARY
Army Form C. 2118.

DADOS 36 Division Vol 16

Place	Date	Hour	Summary of Events and Information	Remarks and references to Appendices
Heio Farm	1/4/17 Sun.		Visit with RE mornings.	
	2/4 Mon.		Sent a lorry to Calais for lunch for 109 Infy Bde. The lorry went intended for after lunch now had gone.	
	3/4 Tues.		Rt Reily for Guide notified, sent. Lorries purchased in afternoon.	
	4/4 Wed.		Major General Pearson was to have visited but did not get time. Lorry ret! from Calais after delivering Books etc to 109: Inf. & 153. Arty Bde. & brought back a load of salvage.	
	5/4 Thurs.		Usual Office routine. 108 Bde. W.O's men moved to Bertaun.	
	6/4 Fri.		W Wo 2 Heavy Morris lorries.	
	7/4 Sat.		office work.	
	8/4 Sun.		Staff car & intended going to Cassel but on route down. Called at 108 Mont Noir. Comparison of issues & necessaries to Bdes shows 109: still heaviest.	

WAR DIARY or INTELLIGENCE SUMMARY

Army Form C. 2118.

Place	Date	Hour	Summary of Events and Information	Remarks and references to Appendices
Idelle Farm	9/4 Mon.		Acting on instruction from "Q", drew 80 shelter from Corps Troops & delivered to 9? Rgt. Inn. Fus. 70 more tents from Base but have had no advice of these. "Q" very slow in Baggage Row, Bailleul.	
	10/4 11.00.		Office in morning. Visited Bath switch A.P.S. in afternoon & talked over matters. departmental.	
	11/4 Wed.		No Soap or Soda from Base this week, as Bath urgently require both endeavoured to purchase in afternoon, succeeded in buying 2 cwt Soda, 500 bars of Soap. 2nd week that Oil Fuel has failed to come up.	
	12/4 Thurs.		Visited 108 Bde. & School of Instruction re equipment for manual also in afternoon 107 Hd. Qrs. & 109 Hd. Qrs.	
	13/4 Fri.		Local purchased in Hazebrouck field for ball clothes washed brushes & 3 cwts yds Tape for instructors in training areas. Went to Calais to arrange about 107 Bde. being supplied direct from there by our own Ordnance lorries.	
	14/4 Sat.			
	15/4 "		There being no Soap & Soda at the Base I ordered locally 1000 bars Sunlight & 500 K.J Soda for the Baths use. Queries on A.B.O's. & Dn. H.D. Qrs.	

Place	Date	Hour	Summary of Events and Information	Remarks and references to Appendices
Hill top Farm Sheet 28 S.9.b.6.5.	16/7		We are awaiting Head Quarters in afternoon from i.e. Q. re next gun book and running short. Office is throwing up its work in taken up keeping track of extra divisions those not calculated this week in their Establishment & has any extra staff been allotted for this work. Receiving & issuing is mainly provision for these we fair known requirements in advance in the field, but the issuing of a small staff into temporary Ordnance rooms is entirely extra & to do full justice to this fair & salvage will in the provision & issue of Ordnance Stores to a Division I feel is a severe strain on a small staff, the consequence is there is no reserve enough left for extra calls.	
	17/7		In office in morning. On Q. Entrenching Bn. producing 9th Corps Q. actg. gave order on Baggage Store to issue 20 tents altho' no word from an "Q". Walken to Arty. units in afternoon.	
	18/7		Wire from "Q" to issue 10 tents to 8th Entrenching Bn, the latter will return 10 to Baggage Store to-day. Maj. Green sick in afternoon.	
	19/7 Thurs.			

WAR DIARY
or
INTELLIGENCE SUMMARY

Army Form C. 2118.

Place	Date	Hour	Summary of Events and Information	Remarks and references to Appendices
Hill Farm	20/4 Fri.		Bought more Soap in Bailleul for the Field Ambulances.	
Sheet 28 SW S.G.B.2404	21/4 Sat.		Went to St. Omer & Hazebrouck endeavouring to purchase material for "G" truck for special purpose but could not get the right things. Will try again at first opportunity. Visited 107th H.Q. but my W.O. had gone to Bailleul for new stores.	
	22/4 Sun.		Walked to one or two neighbouring units in afternoon.	
	23/4 Mon.		Went to Calais had difficulty in obtaining a distinctive yellow material for flags in connection with a future scheme, eventually obtained some in Boulevard de la Fayette.	
	24/4 Tues.		In office all day except for calling in Fd Amb re return of winter clothing.	
	25/4 Wed.		Arranging with Calais to return any winter clothing from BOISENGHEIM area (where 107 Inft Bde) direct to O.O. Receipt Calais by lorry from that area.	
	26/4 Thurs.		Arranged for a dump at METREN for 107th on arrival in that area. Visited units & salvage dumps at Branoutre	

Army Form C. 2118.

WAR DIARY
or
INTELLIGENCE SUMMARY

(Erase heading not required.)

Instructions regarding War Diaries and Intelligence Summaries are contained in F. S. Regs., Part II. and the Staff Manual respectively. Title Pages will be prepared in manuscript.

Place	Date	Hour	Summary of Events and Information	Remarks and references to Appendices
HILLE FARM Sheet 28.S.W. S.9.c.central	27/4		Have had difficulty in obtaining Schrader horn pressure gauges at the Base. Sent up gauges only registering 1800 lbs. & cylinders are charged to 2300 lb. i.e. 1800 Klm. 6 Sep. descents. Base Sent issues from W.O. stating that 1250 lb. pressure is sufficient. Have forwarded through 96 Army the circumstances asking for higher registering gauges as there will ensue in that instance the need for the pressure of air cylinders to be registered at the lowered pressure.	
"	28/4		Sent Conv. 16634 to BOISENGHEIM to assist in return of winter Clo. from 107 Bde. to Calais. To Mont Noir in morning but R.O.P.S. out. Rode in afternoon to Inenstre & unit. Lewis Gun rec'd yesterday for 14 D.L.R. rec. to Base as the one "put out of action" is found to be repairable.	
"	29/4		Office work in morning Called on D.D.O.S. 2nd Army in afternoon	
"	30/4		Received wound want & saw A.D.O.S.	

Winterbage Capt
D.A.D.O.S. 36 Div

Army Form C. 2118.

DADOS.
36th Division

WAR DIARY
or
INTELLIGENCE SUMMARY

(Erase heading not required.)

Instructions regarding War Diaries and Intelligence Summaries are contained in F. S. Regs., Part II. and the Staff Manual respectively. Title Pages will be prepared in manuscript.

Place	Date	Hour	Summary of Events and Information	Remarks and references to Appendices
Hill Farm Sheet 28 S.9.B.cen	1/5/17		Usual office routine, nothing very important	V6117
	2/5/17		Big store tent up from Base for winter clo. arranged by D.D.O.S. having it erected & put up at Raickend. Many Blankets coming in privately on account of very warm weather prevailing.	
	3/5/17		Capt. Mackenzie went on leave. Capt. Castle Officer to Sub-Area – Claims O. will be acting D.A.D.O.S.	
	4/5/17		Conference at 10.30 a.m. under A.A & Q.M.G. for Staff Captains DADOS and other Officers concerned – Subjects discussed, inter alia, Salvage and Returns & Serviceable & unserviceable Articles in relation to indents for the same – Preservation of water – protection against the heading of flies – removal of Winter Clothing – Units may dump same at Store tent at Haegedoorne Siding – Ordnance lorries to carry weekly fares.	

Army Form C. 2118.

WAR DIARY
or
INTELLIGENCE SUMMARY
(Erase heading not required.)

Instructions regarding War Diaries and Intelligence Summaries are contained in F.S. Regs., Part II. and the Staff Manual respectively. Title Pages will be prepared in manuscript.

Place	Date	Hour	Summary of Events and Information	Remarks and references to Appendices
Dick Farm	5/5 Sat.		To Wagenhoek endeavouring to obtain special material for "G." On return is sending to Paris. In accordance with late Army instruction has 2 pits in this camp which have been filled, other steps taken for purification of water. 8/7 am having work-horse effort & during summer.	
	6/5 Sun.		Usual office routine all day. 1500 Respirators from Base. Fly traps, Butter muslin & sprayers on appointed to assist in fly-killing campaign.	
	7/5 Mon.		Usual departmental work all day. D.D.V.S. called in afternoon to ask why truck allotted were not being filled. Salvage queue feel instructions tup the difficulty is in my being able to put actual details in the one truck. 2 Loan Blanket group away to money.	
	8/5 Tues.		Car all day & was able to settle several outstanding matters with 3 a 4 claims. To Wagenhoek & obtained samples of new cloth also had cylinder for Stanhas storm filled at 2 Army Workshops Col. Conger called in morning.	
	9/5 Wed.		Clothing ret. to Salvage Compound with issues sent to "Q." 11 am "D.R." to Div. H.Q. in afternoon & long interview with A.A. & Q.M.G. over several matters. All men in this camp have now been thro. Gas Chamber.	

WAR DIARY
or
INTELLIGENCE SUMMARY.
(Erase heading not required.)

Army Form C. 2118.

Instructions regarding War Diaries and Intelligence Summaries are contained in F. S. Regs., Part II. and the Staff Manual respectively. Title pages will be prepared in manuscript.

Place	Date 1917	Hour Day	Summary of Events and Information	Remarks and references to Appendices
Hell Farm Shut 28.	10/5	Thur.	22,000 Evertrons for Box Respirators arrived from Base & units are being supplied as they submit indents. Distribution of 70 Sprayers for abolition of flies received from "Q".	
S.G.6. central	11/5	Fri.	Col. Corryn visited in evening & wishes slabs made after erected who is being attended to. Car in afternoon to Hazebrouck Field Cashier & for Books Clothing etc from Base today.	
	12/5	Sat.	Advised by "Q" that 450 Shelters will arrive at "Q" Cap Troops Tomorrow for no & given distribution mostly for 107 Bde. who go eastwards with a new camp. To-morrow, will have to find new dump for Bde. W.O. who is now at Metren.	
	13/5	Sun.	Attended conference at A.D.S. office to discuss proposal to have a Gun Park close to this office (shut 28. S.9.B central) as only acting DADOS I have not much knowledge of Ord. routine so took S/C Brennen who was O.C. for 12 months.	
	14/5	Mon.	Shelters did not arrive until mid-day train but were delivered as directed by "Q". Also 3000 Blankets arrived for A.D.m.S. who drew direct from Rhd. 9 Cw of Oats from Base today including 100 Yukon Packs.	

WAR DIARY
or
INTELLIGENCE SUMMARY.
(Erase heading not required.)

Army Form C. 2118.

Place	Date	Hour Day	Summary of Events and Information	Remarks and references to Appendices
Hall Farm	14/5	MON.	Office in morning. Bought Red Paint to Bombing Officer in afternoon. Sent same up to Dranoutre. Round Neuve Eglise neighbourhood on matters connected with claims.	
Sheet 28 Sq 6 Cultac	15/5	TUES.	Most of morning spent at Court-Martial 8" R.I.R. Office in afternoon. Drew 10 30'x20' Covers from "Q" Corps Troops & delivered to Dix Arty. at Daylight Corner as per "Q" instructions.	
	16/5	WED.	To A.D.O.S in afternoon who tell me that all A.D.O.S' are putting up a strong protest to the Army against A.R.O. 809 which states that no further textile stores are to be purchased in France.	
	17/5	THURS.	470 Stretchers arrive for A.D.M.S. who was advised & arranged removal. Tailor finding plenty to do making ambulance flags etc. just at present. 3 Yukon Packs sent to D.D.Q in morning. Saw A.A.Q.M.G. 2" Army in accordance with instructions re' from D.O.S. sent 2 lorries to 2" Army	
	18/5	FRI.	Carrier & drew 5794 Ground Canvas Bucket Patt. 1200 Ground Canvas Bell Patt. 1500 Neil Rulbus Large. Half of these quantities are for 9" C.T. & for 11" Division. Capt. Mackenzie distributed to our 3 Bdes. returned from there this evening.	

WAR DIARY
or
INTELLIGENCE SUMMARY.

Army Form C. 2118.

Place	Date	Hour DAY	Summary of Events and Information	Remarks and references to Appendices
Willi Farm S.9.B.cen.	19/5	SAT.	Office in morning & at Conference at H.Q. Qr.Q. Stores on Salvage question to Sub Area Officer. Local purchase in afternoon.	
	20/5	SUN	Office all morning & evening. To Cassel to see D.D.O.S. Second Army in afternoon.	
	21/5	MON.	Car in morning, Local purchase. Office all afternoon viewing settling several matters.	
	22/5	TUES.	To Dunkirk to purchase rope urgently required for use with improvised packsaddles bought all available – 2500' – more will be ready in a few days. Also bought Buckles, Straw etc. for Saddlers.	

Place	Date	Hour	Summary of Events and Information	Remarks and references to Appendices
Hillstown	23/5	Wed	Visiting units and arranging making up of various appliances for use in offensive.	
	24	Thursday	Trucks have been one day late all this week owing to congestion of traffic. 530 Kirk rivetors & rivets to duty units coming into Area. In each case Kirk was in more than enough for each motorised unit with full directions, but in most cases units ignored directions and asked for more outfits as the method they adopted was wasteful. Kirk should invariably be revetted[?] started from the manufactures & it almost impossible to get units to carry this out properly owing to difficulty of obtaining boiling water in any quantities.	
	25	Fri	Visiting units till 4 P.M. then in the office late.	
	26	Sat	Office till 4 P.M. Visited ADOS and local purchases	

WAR DIARY
INTELLIGENCE SUMMARY
(Erase heading not required.)

Army Form C. 2118.

Place	Date	Hour	Summary of Events and Information	Remarks and references to Appendices
Hill Farm	27/5 Sun		Distinguishing flags for rifle rec'd from Ord. & Armourer corporal adjustment on rifles all packed up, ready for issue to Bttn. tomorrow. Rec'd particulars of the gun wheel will be kept by Gun Park & method to be adopted in indenting. Heavy bombardment appearing to be from this side. Granada, lasting from 9 p.m. to 4 a.m., shell, travelling sounded very close.	
	28/5 Mon		Sent my lorries as early as possible to move Bris. H.Q. Qm. During to enquiries on roads by eastern traffic considers that thing's DYANOUTRES? is not very safe for advanced Ord. Dumps. They had kept/stay there, through return a 8.30	3/5 7/5
	29/5 Tues		S'krein on the bn. shelling of night & move in daytime. Another bad night for the men in D'granite. Saw A.D.O.S. re getting 2 pack cars. Very busy these days with the Quartermaster & Staff Captain	
	30/5 Wed.		Was asked for 100 F.S. Lamps by Hd. Qrs. A.D.O.S. will endeavour to obtain Some but couldn't early supplies up. Ordered 12 2" T Mortars from Corps Troops. Ordnance now cut to	
	31/5 Thurs		Ordnance Extracted all gun parts to Park immediately & will keep 20 in reserve in Park Depot as they have not held any stores for sometime, having been much so much. To A.D.O.S. on horse in morning & busy in office afternoon & evening	

DADOS
36th Division

Vol 18

WAR DIARY

INTELLIGENCE SUMMARY.
(Erase heading not required.)

Army Form C. 2118.

Instructions regarding War Diaries and Intelligence Summaries are contained in F. S. Regs., Part II. and the Staff Manual respectively. Title pages will be prepared in manuscript.

Place	Date	Hour	Summary of Events and Information	Remarks and references to Appendices
Suzanne Farm	1/6 Fri.		Visiting units & ADOs re Arty & T.M. Batteries. Trains very heavy	
	2/6 Sat.		Visiting units in morning & office all rest of day.	
	3/6 Sun.		Called at Army Genl park & A.D.O.S. & 11 Div HQ & to see their Q as their D.A.D.O.S is away & I promised to call when I could. Visited 109 Infy Bde.	
	4/6		Anytown in morning to local furniture visited ind.	
	5/6		This morning an Ammunition train on line was hit by bomb & the pieces fell all round my dump all morning from the explosion	

Army Form C. 2118.

WAR DIARY
or
INTELLIGENCE SUMMARY.
(Erase heading not required.)

Instructions regarding War Diaries and Intelligence Summaries are contained in F. S. Regs., Part II. and the Staff Manual respectively. Title pages will be prepared in manuscript.

Place	Date	Hour	Summary of Events and Information	Remarks and references to Appendices
Helle	6/6 (cont)		Called on the A.D.O.S. & Army Gun Park in afternoon. Officers were having difficulty in obtaining barrels for Vickers guns & several urgent quests re gun stores. So went to Calais in evening arriving there at 9.30 PM	
	6/6		Went into question re intake of T.M. parts est in morning & cleared up many points. Everything in good order for the offensive only one 18 pr due to artly, which I expect tomorrow to draw from Gun Park any moment. The Division went over the lot everything not successful, only one Vickers gun reported as a casualty. No 18 pr or 4.5" (How) all guns now in action having drawn the only outstanding one the morning. Sent out lorries with Cuffers cart to take up drum wagon drawn trench & waterproof sheets to the 10 q Infy Bde. Not much salvage received yet by Divising Salvage	
	7/6			

WAR DIARY
or
INTELLIGENCE SUMMARY.

Army Form C. 2118.

Place	Date	Hour	Summary of Events and Information	Remarks and references to Appendices
Hell Farm	8/6 Fri		Very busy with salvage ret. equipment deficiencies of 108 & 108 Infy Bde in out items of equipment from articles salted from line while they were still in the trenches. Orders to move to St Denis.	
	9/6 Sat		Arranged exchange of Dumps with 118th Div but have had orders since that 9 will now stay where I am.	
	10/6 Sun		Delay in obtaining Dial Sight No 7, new ADOS who has sent us to Gun Park where supply had just arrived & was able to bring one away & hand one direct to Battery. 32 Div. Arty. returning to XIV Corps. Pocketadilly being returned in again. My Bdes who had extra for the offensive. Tents also being returned. Require far larger staff for reissuing. Received 7 German machine guns from units.	

Army Form C. 2118.

WAR DIARY
or
INTELLIGENCE SUMMARY.
(Erase heading not required.)

Instructions regarding War Diaries and Intelligence Summaries are contained in F. S. Regs., Part II. and the Staff Manual respectively. Title pages will be prepared in manuscript.

Place	Date	Hour	Summary of Events and Information	Remarks and references to Appendices
Hill Farm	11/6	MON	Very busy day reviewing returned tents, and stores from Base which had been delayed on line, driving Park again & checking returns of penaddlery etc coming in & if these were to continue & would require a much larger staff. Three German M. Guns received & being painted with captors names.	
	12/6	TUE	Visited 107 & 108 Bde much difference not exercising particularly in 108 Inf Bde. went round Forward Salvage & found most of the heifer material picked up. Still many shell cases about & 2" T.M. bombs which were tried to explode.	
	13/6	WED.	Maj Green Staff Capt. here in afternoon to inspect & decide on captured M. Guns, these are all to be sent up to Corps H.Q. Attendant Rec'd method of how supplies from Gun Park have worked.	
			wire to attend conference at A.D.O.S. tomorrow to discuss	
	14/6	THUR	Gn 108 MG Bn moving, I had to send a W.O. to do Sgt. if 2 Bns as gave him a Sgt. also as right hand. B.W. W.O. at Dranoutre will as All Arty. Engineer & Pioneers. Much buck & detail for 22 Arty will be re-consigned at first opportunity. Continue to make up units from Salvage within. over 170 magazines 2 G. a few Lewis T.m. Canvas Carriers. Visited new 108 MG Dump just outside Dentien.	

WAR DIARY
or
INTELLIGENCE SUMMARY.
(Erase heading not required.)

Army Form C. 2118.

Place	Date 1917	Hour	Summary of Events and Information	Remarks and references to Appendices
Hill Farm Sheet 28 S 9 B central	16/6 Fri.		Have now 7 Ann"s in Shop & they are all very well employed dealing with the rifles & bicycles which are coming in.	
	16/6 Sat.		Col. Comyn (A.D.Q.M.G.) here in morning & explained to him how stores & equipt. have been collected from Salvage & gone a long way towards making units up again. Gives intimation of a move by Div. to Menin area. Visited Depôt on horse to enquire what is to be done with reserve stores, all special close being asked for such as Packsaddles, Canvas Amm. Yukon Jacks etc. which it is impossible for me to take.	
	17/6 Sun		Cleared to D.O. 1X Corps Hdqtrs. all surplus special stores & made ready to move on 18th inst. Arranged to leave survey party under Freeman & his staff to look after Div. Area. R.E. Coys. After all arrangement made with for leaving tomorrow, wire rec'd from "D." 9 pm Cancelling the move.	

Army Form C. 2118.

WAR DIARY
or
INTELLIGENCE SUMMARY.
(Erase heading not required.)

Instructions regarding War Diaries and Intelligence Summaries are contained in F. S. Regs., Part II. and the Staff Manual respectively. Title pages will be prepared in manuscript.

Place	Date	Hour	Summary of Events and Information	Remarks and references to Appendices
Hill 19 Farm	18/6	MON.	Division will not move back but is taking our line from 11"-19". 2 Divs. will have attacks to no Arty. of the former. Went to "Q" in morning. 8 Ottawa battalion will probably have to move to Dranoutre in a day or two. Col. Thos (AOD) called in afternoon. I was interested in Salvage methods.	
	19/6	TUE.	Obtained a certain amount of underclothing etc. to commence Loan Baths etc. Drew 100 Yukon packs from Corps Troops for 107 Bde. Base for 3000 more suits.	
	20/6	WED.	Usual daily routine. car in afternoon visited one or two units to Kemmel to arrange a suitable dump for Ordnance issues.	
	21/6	THUR	11th Divnl Arty. are attached to me temporarily for Ordnance but with a Sgt. & a man left behind to look after this does not mean very much extra work. Bde. WD of 107 Bde. went to Kemmel to administer to his units. 108, 109 Bde. remain at Dranoutre. My office to remain at Hill Farm.	

WAR DIARY
or
INTELLIGENCE SUMMARY.

(Erase heading not required.)

Army Form C. 2118.

Place	Date	Hour	Summary of Events and Information	Remarks and references to Appendices
Hell Farm	22/6	FRI.	Saw A.D.O.S. re Div. Only if Div. were to separate not making separate mess but returning stores by lorry.	
	23/6	SAT.	Instructed by A.D.O.S. to take on 12 2" T. Mortars issued for Special Operation took them to his disposal. Visited 108 Inf Bde + M.G. Coy + 109 Inf Bde H.Q.	
	24/6	SUN.	The 107 Suffolks M.G. Coy left a Barn & Shrows range finder with T. Betty Ant: aircraft while they were attached on May 3. 1917. This was to be repaired & they had not heard of it. I found the A.A. Battery who had applied for a new one or an I.O.M.S. Certificate to be forwarded to M.G. Coy. Above Items to IX Corps will have it transferred to 30 Div.	
	25/6	MON.	Usual daily routine. Visited on a two unit at Kemmel where Dump has been much raided with Shrapnel. Div. will move to Merris area shortly & will be relieved by 37. Division.	

WAR DIARY
INTELLIGENCE SUMMARY
(Erase heading not required.)

Army Form C. 2118.

Place	Date	Hour	Summary of Events and Information	Remarks and references to Appendices
Hee Farm	26/6 TUES		Visits paid to where 3rd Class C 150 are now coming up & urgently required have hastened the Base but stock there out.	
	27/6 WED		Arranged to hand over to 1 X Corps Troops the surplus stores held for Munirons.	
	28/6 THURS		Drew 8 Lewis Gun A.A. mountings from R.E. Workshop, Hazebrouck - 4 for 107 Bde - 4 for 109 Bde. Mar DAQMG & MERRIS saw ADOS re 112 Div Arty Stores due yesterday (Oil Grease, Equipt, Picketing Gear etc.) Got up yesterday failed to turn up again to-day, owing to very heavy train.	
	29/6 FRI.		Sent in advance party with reserve stores to take over dump at MERRIS. Visited new dump. Transferred 112 Div Arty to 112 Div. Transferred 121, 122, 150 Field Coys. & 6 R.P.(?) to 5th Army.	
	30/6 SAT.		Moved to Merris & cleared everything from Here Farm. Our lorry & a Sgt. & man at Dranoutre to look after Artillery	

DADOS
36" Div"
Vol/9

Army Form C. 2118.

WAR DIARY
or
INTELLIGENCE SUMMARY.
(Erase heading not required.)

Place	Date	Hour	Summary of Events and Information	Remarks and references to Appendices
Merris	1/7/17 SUN		Visited ADOS IX Corps & hung in office all day. Have not much room for too accomodation but can manage temporarily.	
	2/7 MON		St Omer to local purchase materials for repair of crates. Drew stores from Bailleul. Received a good very nearly all to units.	
	3/7 TUES		Visited Div Amn in morning. Mess in afternoon. Am transferring all outstanding gun stores from Gun Park to Base on moving to 5th Army. Instruction to this effect rec'd from 9th Corps to-day.	
	4/7 WED		Arty Stores Aus-out extracted from above list sent to DADOS 55 Dn for them to submit indent to 5: Army Gun Park as the Arty are now definitely in 5th Army.	
	5/7 THURS		Visited Wizernes & arranged for Dump & office, not very much room for dump. Also saw D.D.O.S. 5th Army. Yesterday truck of air cases, pickling gear etc. arrived at Caestre but as units moved to-day it would be useless to draw will endeavour to haul rec consigned to St Omer.	

WAR DIARY
or
INTELLIGENCE SUMMARY.

(Erase heading not required.)

Army Form C. 2118.

Place	Date	Day	Summary of Events and Information	Remarks and references to Appendices
MERRIS	6/7	FRI.	As we shall in all probability only be down the line for a week or so, it is hardly worth while carting round of Gas Appliances etc. so I have sent 3 lorry loads to Thieu Farm. Left a man in charge to be collected upon our return to front.	
	7/7	SAT.	Cleared all from Merris to Wizernes by 9 a.m.	
WIZERNES	8/7	SUN.	Units very much scattered in this area & our dumps difficulty in getting occupying dumps, consequently majority of store have to be taken round straight from lorry. Visited Bde. with R.A.Q.M.G. in morning.	
	9/7	MON.	Usual daily routine endeavour to find a more spacious store for my dump. D.D.O.S. VIII Corps called in afternoon to acquaint himself with our method of working.	
	10/7	TUES.	Question of 2 18pdr Gun Axles-out to B/153 not clear with Army. I showed there on my Axles-out list to Calais on leaving 2nd Army Park. Calais say obtain from 5" Gun Park but they have no authority to issue am in communication with D.D.O.S. on subject.	

Army Form C. 2118.

WAR DIARY
or
INTELLIGENCE SUMMARY.
(Erase heading not required.)

Place	Date	Hour Day	Summary of Events and Information	Remarks and references to Appendices
WIZERNES	11/7	WED.	Notification received from Corps that we now come under Appendix Schedule for inducting in back, & alterations out Div.H.Q. for a D.R. to be published for units. Information On in afternoon visited one or two units on tour.	S/c Sallie on tour.
	12/7	THURS.	Permission given for to-day to be a general holiday as far as poss.	
	13/7	FRI.	Upon instructions rec'd from Col. Comps. sent lorry to Reserve Clos at Thees Farm to draw 50 crates for Jack Saddles.	
	14/7	SAT.	Usual daily routine.	
	15/7	SUN.	Administrative instructions rec'd from Div. as to use of Jackasadlery throughout Div. "Rope Ruts & Bolts will be obtained from D.A.D.O.S."	
	14/7	MON.	Instructions rec'd to return all Arm'd Staff Sgts. to units except one of 15th R.R. Complied with. To Boulogne in morning & purchased 600 metres of Rope some Rings for Bolts for fitting of Jackasadlery. Office in afternoon. Transferred all dues-out of M.G. D.F.W.L) park to 5" Army Gun Park.	

WAR DIARY
or
INTELLIGENCE SUMMARY.
(Erase heading not required.)

Army Form C. 2118.

Place	Date	Hour	Summary of Events and Information	Remarks and references to Appendices
WIZERNES	17/7	Tue.	In accordance with instructions rec'd from "G" the 3" Stokes Mortar (instructions) which I had is to be sent to OO. 9th Corps troops at Canada Corner. The	
(HAZEBROUCK 5A)			will be done by first available lorry tomorrow morning same lorry will bring back more crates for Bomb Shop who are working on these.	
	18/7	Wed.	To Boulogne again in morning ordered more Rope brought more Rings. Delivered 300 metres of Rope previously bought to 108 Bde.	
	19/7	Thur.	Usual office routine. Am receiving many enquiries to make units up to establishment.	
	20/7	Fri.	Vortex units in morning, find everything very satisfactory. By two water Carts due - out (109 M.G.C. & 10 R.R.) Base say will be issued as soon as available, they are being reserved for special purpose just now. HQ informed of this.	
	21/7	Sat.	Col. Purdy I.D.G.T. Corps came round to whom we now come under for administration, discussed matters departmental in general. # ton Packing Gear etc. from Base issued in afternoon by lorries.	

Army Form C. 2118.

WAR DIARY
or
INTELLIGENCE SUMMARY.
(Erase heading not required.)

Instructions regarding War Diaries and Intelligence Summaries are contained in F.S. Regs., Part II. and the Staff Manual respectively. Title pages will be prepared in manuscript.

Place	Date	Hour	Summary of Events and Information	Remarks and references to Appendices
WIZERNES (HAZEBROUCK 5A)	22/7 Sun.		Office in morning and seeing units in afternoon.	
	23/7 Mon.		First load of M.G. parts arrive from Gun Park & leave very little outstanding to units. Boulogne to local purchase in morning.	
	24/7 Tues		Visiting units of 9, 10 & Infy Bde & 15g Infy Bde.	
	25/7 Wed.		Calais in morning. Inspd. Chop & Store to Winnezeele in afternoon.	
WINNEZEELE Sheet 27 J.17.A.5.9.	26/7 Thur		Brig. H.Q. moved to WINNEZEELE & my office.	
	27/7 Fri.		To Adot. 5th Army in morning & drew 94 Companies magnetos which compell units to recall. Units are crying out for C/o. Books. Truck was due on two, but owing to move it was re-consigned & has not yet arrived at new Railhead, should certainly be up tomorrow.	

A6945. Wt. W.11422/M1160. 35,000 12/16 D.D.&I. Forms/C/2118/14.

WAR DIARY
or
INTELLIGENCE SUMMARY.
(Erase heading not required.)

Army Form C. 2118.

Place	Date	Hour Day	Summary of Events and Information	Remarks and references to Appendices
WINNE- ZEELE	28/7/17	SAT.	To Cassel in morning obtained one or two articles which were urgently required. Also purchased iron etc. for converting eratio.	
	29/7/17	SUN.	In office all day clearing a large amount of paper work accumulated yesterday. A.D.O.S. XIX Corps called in evening & discussed with him our methods of working. Rec'd 2400 Bucket Patt. Grenade Covers from Base which complete B.no. to further 200 each authorised by G.R.O.	
	30/7/17	MON.	My office moved to POPERINGHE with Divnl H.Q. Dumps will move to WATOU area tomorrow when Bues. are.	
POPER- INGHE	31/7/17	TUES.	Visited all dumps in morning & established dump at each Res. Bn Qrs. Called in this Armourer with "Q"'s permission as too much accumulated for 1 to deal with. A.D.O.S. called in morning.	

Churchley Capt
D.A.D.O.S. 31 Div.

DADOS
36th Division

Vol 20

WAR DIARY
INTELLIGENCE SUMMARY
(Erase heading not required.)

Army Form C. 2118.

Place	Date	Hour Day	Summary of Events and Information	Remarks and references to Appendices
POPER -INGHE	1/8/17	WED.	Have arranged suitable place for Armrs Shop. Called in 3 more Armourer Staff Sgts.	
	2/8/17	THURS.	Division is relieving 55th Div. in line it will therefore be necessary to call in the Bttn. from Watou area. 107 W.O. arrived here today. Car in evening. Sgt. managed a little local purchase, wire for making security boxs for Burial Officer.	
	3/8/17	FRI.	Visited all Bttns. in morning & found everything satisfactory. 108 & 109 have been issued with crate irons & 107 wired to draw today. First arrangement of N.C. Box Regulators from Base for issue to drafts & reinforcements. 109 W.O. here.	
	4/8/17	SAT.	Divnl. HQ. are moving today up the line but my office is to remain behind in Pop. for time being. To Micrey Camp. (H.1.A.5.6.)	
	5/8/17	SUN	Made arrangements with D.A.D.O.S. 55 Div. to take over his Camp on departure. Also some of his reserve stock including P.H. Helmets, Greatcoats etc.	
	6/8/17	MON.	Moved to 55 Div. Camp at A 25 D 5.3 with my three Dvrs. visited Bttns. & Divnl. H.O.	

WAR DIARY
or
INTELLIGENCE SUMMARY.
(Erase heading not required.)

Army Form C. 2118.

Place	Date	Hour	Summary of Events and Information	Remarks and references to Appendices
TEN ELMS CAMP	7/17	TUES	55 Divl Arty moved to XIX Corp Troops & the like over 61st Divl Arty for administration in exchange	
	8/17	WED.	Rec'd 500 WATSON Signalling Lamps from Corps Troops & asked Q for distribution. Also asked for details of 10,400 rifle magazine arrived from Base yesterday	
	9/17	THURS	Office is moving but we gone to S.O. Owen when DDOS called at 12 A.M. for head Purchases. I have explained having gunny to Proverbs living in mud clothing & 107 Bde just out of the line is a bad state Sent 10g Infy Bde 112R from Div 61st Divs Arty SIGN exp 36 Div Arty and sent Div bid.	
	10/17	FRI		
	11/17	SAT.	Exceptionally heavy office work and demands for stores	
	12/		Work increasing more than before any offensive we have been in	

WAR DIARY or INTELLIGENCE SUMMARY

Army Form C. 2118.

Place	Date	Hour DAY	Summary of Events and Information	Remarks and references to Appendices
Tyee	13th	Mon.	Church parade. Equipment and Rifles Sun very heavy 61st Div	
Elmo Camp A 25 D 5 3	14th	Tues.	Arty demands abnormal but intend to see all Batteries had all Battery Q.M.S. and the Staff Capt. One great difficulty they have in getting means of for washing clothing. There is now the need and many new apparently have been unable to change for 3 to 4 weeks	
"	15th	Wed	Visited all units of 108 Bde in morning & 2 Corp every thing Satisfactory. Delivered Barrels to 109 M.G.C. at Vlamertinghe. Wire Cutters to Bde. Also late at night Division went into the attack complete in all respects as regards Ordnance. ADOS called in evening – discussed course to be taken in regard to special store if we move.	
"	16th	Thur		
"	17th	Fri	Visited Divnl. H.Q. Losses have been heavy, equipment material will be equally heavy. We are being relieved by 6th Div. DADOS here tomorrow.	
Winnezeele	18th	Sat.	Moved office rail Ram. Lro's to Winnezeele. Ammunition will come along tomorrow. Left Sgt. Ichua with Artillery as previously transferred all due out from Elm Park of 36th Hd. 6th Div Arty to DADOS 61st Div.	

WAR DIARY
or
INTELLIGENCE SUMMARY

Army Form C. 2118.

Place	Date	Hour	Summary of Events and Information	Remarks and references to Appendices
WINNEZEELE	19/8/17	SUN.	Received information that move south to 3rd Army in a few days. A.A.! A.M.G. instructs all units to dump their salvage at Bou. HQ. ascertain time where I am to collect with lorries. Visited Bdes. made appointments for all Q.M.'s to meet Bde. W.O.'s to obtain complete list of deficiencies.	
"	20/8/17	MON.	Cancelled all dues-out from Catain Barn who will transfer to Havre. Arranged for units to send in special stores which belong to this Army such as Clinometers, Crates etc.	
"	21/8/17	TUES.	Upon notification that 9 R.I.R. are to be drafted I sent 107 Bde. W.O. to collect all their mob. equipment which will take a considerable time. Went to Catain in Afternoon obtained an order urgently required by 150 Field Coy. List of units deficiencies almost complete	
"	22/8/17	WED.	Collected mob - equipment of 8 & 9 R.I. Rifles showing units deficiencies & wired for 38 Lewis Guns to cover Div.	
	23/8/17	THURS.	Heavy salvage & kit of Casualties very heavy during week indent cancelled all outstanding from Gen. Force limited for 3 Vickers for 109 M.G Coy.	
	24/8/17		and 4 Light T.M. (3" Stokes) for 107 T.M.B., 38 Lewis guns, 9th R. & 9th Jn. F.	

WAR DIARY or INTELLIGENCE SUMMARY

Army Form C. 2118.

(Erase heading not required.)

Instructions regarding War Diaries and Intelligence Summaries are contained in F. S. Regs., Part II. and the Staff Manual respectively. Title Pages will be prepared in manuscript.

Place	Date	Hour	Summary of Events and Information	Remarks and references to Appendices
	23rd	Continue	11 R. Irish Rifles 7. 12 R Irish Rifles 6. 13th R Irish Rifles	
			8. 11 R. Irish Fus. 6. 14 Royal Irish Fus. 4 to replace loss.	
			4 Staff Serv. Moved 16 R. Irish Rifles to 18 Corps Troops, as informers	
			could be definitely obtain as to what Corps in Third Army they were to	
			be attached. Moved to Third Army.	
Dernancourt	24th	10 A.M.	Ammunition Shop & Div Reserve loaded on Trains for Third Army Area remain-	
O.21.D.1.4			-aining by lorry.	
Sheet 57 C		6 P.M.	Officers opened in new area	
O.21.D.1.4	25th		Wired to 4 Vickers for 107 M.G. Coy. The delay in indenting due to endeavour	
			to find out what was still serviceable and what on move.	
	26th		Received all Vickers & known indents for on 28-	

Army Form C. 2118.

WAR DIARY
or
INTELLIGENCE SUMMARY

(Erase heading not required.)

Instructions regarding War Diaries and Intelligence Summaries are contained in F. S. Regs., Part II. and the Staff Manual respectively. Title Pages will be prepared in manuscript.

Place	Date	Hour	Summary of Events and Information	Remarks and references to Appendices
	26		Received 1 x 4 Vickers guns due to 107 Bde M.G. Coy.	
	27		9th Divisional Artillery moved to 36 Div today. Received 1 x 4 section 3" due to 109 T.M.B.	
	28		South Corps Reinforts Station moved to 36 Div and 9th Bett Canteen Railway Troops.	
Sheet 57° O 23 d 54	29		All Vickers Lewis & T.M.s received that were due.	
	30		I have had notice to Vickers even today from 9th Div Ordnance kemp. Am holding standing in Camp and hones friens wind to put up Marquees in	
	31		Store filling in turn have all on metro supplies in two days consequently considerable congestion externally difficult to keep going on these reserves with since stop.	

Mackenzie Cpl
OBOS 36 Div

Army Form C. 2118.

WAR DIARY
or
INTELLIGENCE SUMMARY

(Erase heading not required.)

DADOS
36th Division

Place	Date	Hour	Summary of Events and Information	Remarks and references to Appendices
Bus	1/9/17		Visited unit, and laying out a camp here	
"	2/9/17		Made out report on amalgamation of 8/9 Royal Irish Rifles for XIX Corps.	
"	3rd		Visited units and gun parks. Officers were	
"	4th		Camp gradually taking shape but in short handed and all fences of convenience now up. Hope to improve them later	
"	6th		Routes with lessening were formed the light bees railway in transport, Great pushing in Divin. a great saving	

2449 Wt. W4957/Mgo 750,000 1/16 J.B.C. & A. Forms/C.2118/12.

WAR DIARY or INTELLIGENCE SUMMARY

Army Form C. 2118.

(Erase heading not required.)

Place	Date	Hour	Summary of Events and Information	Remarks and references to Appendices
Bus	9.9.17		Capt. Mackenzie A.O.D. on leave, Lieut. J.A. Moger Dvl. Labour Officer answering for him.	
do	10.9.17		Office routine work. O.O. Boys troops sent up 19 no. of gum boots shot in 1500. Spoke to him about this.	
do	11.9.17		First drafts arrived 10100 taken over by us & commenced issue to Infantry. Started working-party employed firing up Camps.	
do	12.9.17		Office Routine Work. Approaches to camp fixed up & wired.	
do	13.9.17		Local purchases in Albert	
do	15.9.17		Stores collected & sent in area & delivery to Corps Troops, Bapaume.	
do	16.9.17		Office Routine Work.	

WAR DIARY
INTELLIGENCE SUMMARY
(Erase heading not required.)

Army Form C. 2118.

Place	Date	Hour	Summary of Events and Information	Remarks and references to Appendices
Base G.	7/9		Office Routine Work. A.D.O.S. II Corps visited camp. Letter from Army outlining Winter Clothing. Vests Drawers & Pants Bags may be demanded	
"	18"		Local purchases in Albert billed with I.O.M. for T.M. for once. 107" T.M.B.	
"	19"		Office most of the day nothing very particular to report. Gum Boots Thigh to hand.	1500 prs
"	20"		Issued 10,000 Blankets for Winter have been obtained by IV Corps Troops issued as far as possible to Inf. Bns. on reserve of 1 pr. per man.	
"	21"		Capt. Mackenzie returned from leave. $20750 Drawers W. & 12000 Vests received from Base - first consignment of Winter kit.	
"	22"		Demanded further 5500 Blankets to complete to 1 per man. In Office most of day agreeing up queries.	
"	23"		16" R.I.R. returned from 9" Division - more equipment to day. 21 Hot Food Containers demanded.	

Army Form C. 2118.

WAR DIARY
or
INTELLIGENCE SUMMARY

(Erase heading not required.)

Instructions regarding War Diaries and Intelligence Summaries are contained in F. S. Regs., Part II. and the Staff Manual respectively. Title Pages will be prepared in manuscript.

Place	Date	Hour	Summary of Events and Information	Remarks and references to Appendices
Bus	24/9/17	Mon.	Further 1000 Blankets demanded to complete to 1 pr man — 16 R.I.R. Visited Div. H.Q. units.	
	25/9/17	Tues.	In this Army we have to draw our gun stores from Gun Park, army goes about twice a week, not very much outstanding.	Gun Park, army Steward
	26/9/17	Wed.	Local purchase in morning & to school in afternoon. Pair Horse Clipping Machine received from in accordance with O.Ro 2595.	20
	27/9/17	Thurs.	First consignment of Horse Rugs received from Base — 2664. Am endeavouring to obtain African Dust from R.E. for store where we in winter as magneto women give much trouble when stormy weather commences.	Gun All w.o
	28/9/17	Fri.	To Amien. — Local purchase including Irons which Base will not supply saying the authority is exclusive to 2nd Army.	
	29/9/17	Sat.	In office all day, not very much worrying these days except regular daily flow of indents.	
	30/9/17	Sun.	Hot Food Containers rec'd. Hours as per "O" instructions :- 7 to 10½ 14 — 10½	Bee 107 Bee 109 Capt DADOS 36 Div

Whitley

2449 Wt. W14957/M90 750,000 1/16 J.B.C. & A. Forms/C.2118/12.

WAR DIARY
or
INTELLIGENCE SUMMARY

Army Form C. 2118.

WANTS 362
of 22

Place	Date	Hour Day	Summary of Events and Information	Remarks and references to Appendices
Bus.	1/10/17	Mon.	Visited Div. H.Q. in morning & secured several matters with A. & Q.M.G.	
	2/10/17	Tues.	Usual routine. Armourers Rept very busy just now with big number of Bicycles coming in & making night lamps from pieces tins showing route for H.Q.	
	3/10/17	Wed.	In office most of day. Further 2400 Blankets up which completed Div. to 1 per man. A.D.O.S. - Col. Moulton-Barrett called in afternoon.	
	4/10/17	Thurs.	To Amiens. Locat purchased a number of articles which have been asked for during past two weeks.	
	5/10/17	Fri.	Usual routine.	
	6/10/17	Sat.	" " . Stormy weather continues & marquees do well to withstand same. A hut for store is badly needed.	

Army Form C. 2118.

WAR DIARY
or
INTELLIGENCE SUMMARY

(Erase heading not required.)

Instructions regarding War Diaries and Intelligence Summaries are contained in F.S. Regs., Part II. and the Staff Manual respectively. Title Pages will be prepared in manuscript.

Place	Date	Hour Day	Summary of Events and Information	Remarks and references to Appendices
Bus (Somme)	7/10/17	SUN.	Visited A.O.S. in afternoon to correct several matters departmental. Corps inquire if we want any French Overbank Mountings, replied to "Q" Corp. Reinforcement Camp taken on for Administration. Army to run park also took Am: Sect for duty there.	
	8/10/17	MON.	Demanded 12 Rifles with Telescopic Sight to complete under G.R.O. 3059. Nothing of importance to record.	
	9/10/17	TUES.	Attended conference of Staff Capts. at "Q" in morning. Subject re-inforcements not being fully equipped — DAQ are writing to Base to effect improvement if pos.	
	10/10/17	WED.	No car available, have a number of little things awaiting. Drew 20 French 1.5 Overbank Mtgs. from 56: Division approval given (3" ARO 1143) for 50 Soyer Stoves per Div the winter, "Q" say we are in possession of this number.	
	11/10/17	THUR.	Office all day, usual routine.	
	12/10/17	FRI.	To Amiens all day local purchase. A.O.S. called whilst away, phoned him in evening.	

Army Form C. 2118.

WAR DIARY
or
INTELLIGENCE SUMMARY

(Erase heading not required.)

Instructions regarding War Diaries and Intelligence Summaries are contained in F. S. Regs., Part II. and the Staff Manual respectively. Title Pages will be prepared in manuscript.

Place	Date	Hour	Summary of Events and Information	Remarks and references to Appendices
Bus (Somme)	13/10/19 Sat.		Commenced building a winter store next the Decauville siding as this does not appear to be any immediate prospect of receiving an Airman Hut.	
	14/10/19 Sun.			
	15/10/19 Mon.		Had long conversation with Staff Capt. 109 Bde. respecting change of underclothing for troops recent big demands by some of the Bn. unit.	
	16/10/19 Tues.			
	17/10/19 Wed.		Remained in Field Amb. all day with slight ptomaine poisoning.	
	18/10/19 Thur.		Usual routine in office all day. Find it necessary to cut down certain units demands when as many Jackets as Trousers are indented for a Jacket should serve as long as two pairs of Trousers.	

Army Form C. 2118.

WAR DIARY
or
INTELLIGENCE SUMMARY

(Erase heading not required.)

Instructions regarding War Diaries and Intelligence Summaries are contained in F. S. Regs., Part II. and the Staff Manual respectively. Title Pages will be prepared in manuscript.

Place	Date	Hour	Summary of Events and Information	Remarks and references to Appendices
E.Run? (Somme)	19/10/17	FRI.	Went to Amiens with several other passengers on account of whose purchases was unable to obtain all I required them being no room. 2" Blanket per man commenced to arrive from Base	(5+6) being
	20/10/17	SAT.	Capt. Gale A.D arrived from Havre to enclendudy D.A.D.O.S work.	
	21/10/17	SUN.	Sent 1 Am: Staff-Sgt. to A.A.O. 3rd Army for temp. duty as per instructions from Corps. Visited Rhd in afternoon. 1.18 p.m. board arrived from Calais but no orders of number went Bari for the So 3 clue out	
	22/10/17	MON.	Col. Comyn D.A.A.G called in morning. Inspected several examples of clothing being used by units as underneath some of which to go up for the General's inspection.	A/153.
	23/10/17	TUES.	Office all day. WAA Staff Capt R.A concerning a Ry. who was working S.O. for Oat Sacks as they could not obtain more Bags, all demands for these latter have been met promptly for many months. Sent 18 p.m. thank to join to be fitted for A/153.	
	24/10/17	WED.	Went through all papers over with Capt. Gale. Visited units	
	25/10/17			

WAR DIARY
or
INTELLIGENCE SUMMARY

(Erase heading not required.)

Army Form C. 2118.

Place	Date	Hour	Summary of Events and Information	Remarks and references to Appendices
	26/11		Issue Punctured a Capt Gale returned to Havre	
	27/11		Two F.S. men arrived from Base to replace Category A men. These were evidently picked out the Ptes Pheese & Pheene but apparently excellent men but no previous training in civil or military life to particularly fit them as Storemen	
	28/11		Visited 105 + 107 Infty Bdes. & HQ Qn.	
	29/11		Ammunition returned from inspection of 109 Bde Ammn report all cround went to Army Heavy Mobile Workshops re clothing which had not been satisfactory	
	30/11		87 Bde HQ QRE & 466 + 467 & 401st Field Cos RE 1st/8th Royal Scots Pioneers arrived from 51 Div.	
	31/12		Visited unit & A.D.O.S. IV Corps.	

Mawberger Capt.
DADOS 36 Div.

WAR DIARY Army Form C. 2118.
or
INTELLIGENCE SUMMARY

(Erase heading not required.)

Place	Date	Hour Day	Summary of Events and Information	Remarks and references to Appendices
Bus (Somme)	1/7	Thurs.	Hdqs opened line for water-carrying parties from Base, "Q" asked for distribution. 1/6 a/b Packartillery which was ret'd to Base some weeks ago by instructions from "Q" are again from Base & sent into 3. Army troops in accordance with instructions from S.O.1. IV Corps.	
	2/7	Fri.	In office all day nothing very out of ordinary to relate. Which demands all very normal just now.	
	3/7	Sat.	11,500 ord Jenkins & Tea Carts arrived either will be mixed complete Infantry to-morrow. To Amiens all day, considerable A.P. to be done.	
	4/7	Sun.	Office all morning worked in afternoon.	
	5/7	Mon.	To Divnl Hd. in morning had interview with M Col. Green, new A.A.& Q.M.G. who wrote my office to move to Div. H.Q. Still had to remain at Bus. 1 Ord P.B. man air from 56 Div. another to come enter. Visited Army H.Q. in morning & many W'shops to collect Clipper heads. Got called at camp where I was away long to deliver in afternoon drew gun stores.	

Army Form C. 2118.

WAR DIARY
or
INTELLIGENCE SUMMARY

(Erase heading not required.)

Instructions regarding War Diaries and Intelligence Summaries are contained in F.S. Regs., Part II. and the Staff Manual respectively. Title Pages will be prepared in manuscript.

Place	Date	Hour	Summary of Events and Information	Remarks and references to Appendices
Bus (Somme)	7/7/17 Wed.		18 pdr. gun taken to Bm. Bapaume for adjustment for M/743.	
	8/7/17 Thurs		Usual daily routine with more incidents than average today.	
	9/7/17 Fri.		My office moved to Dure. to Ytres Dump remain in at Bus.	
	10/7/17 Sat.	1000	Sixteen Amb. drawn from Corps Troops issued to 108" Field Amb. also 3000 Blankets to be drawn for same unit to-morrow. 1,200 Yukon Packs 1,124 Ords. Packs Jackets, Leather to be issued in accordance with new distribution of Divnl. Pack Transport issued by D?	
	11/7/17 Sun		Arranged to go to Amiens yesterday but on arrangements to upon going in this morning found all business places closed. First consignment of F.S. Book received from Bure.	

Place	Date	Hour	Summary of Events and Information	Remarks and references to Appendices
Ytres (Somme)	12/7/17 MON.	DAY	One of my clerks left for transfer to Infantry. Went to Amiens & obtained all requirements including Range Rods for Coy. and with Orde. Large quantity of kit which to obtain.	
	13/7/17 TUE.		Visits all Brigades. Arrangements to take over mortar stores of 13th R.F.A. & transferred to 60 Corps Troops. 11 R.I.R. Rifles and 13th RVR. delivered new used 11/13 R.F. Rifles & rechange 13/19 ing inst. Saw T.M.B. 10th S.H. Regt. 2nd R.R. arrived divnl area from 25th Divn.	
	14/7/17 WED.			
	15/7/17 THURS.		Visits 2nd & R.F. Rifles and 108 Infy Bde.	
	16/7/17 FRI.		Railhead from to-day is Bapaume in consequence of big Armand or Decauville for other purposes. No mixed instructions for all units to draw Ordnance from Bns in future. Further 209 V.Packs from R. from to-day Lovis to take over Adv. Gun Store issue spare drill to Bdys. I am only to demand upon I.Om instructions. 135 Junts (post 209) drawn from Corps Troops.	
	17/7/17 SAT.			
	18/7/17 SUN		Went to Corps Gun Park in morning & drew B.M. Sight urgently required by C/143 which were officered from gun recently received. One misunderstanding.	

Army Form C. 2118.

WAR DIARY
or
INTELLIGENCE SUMMARY
(Erase heading not required.)

Instructions regarding War Diaries and Intelligence Summaries are contained in F.S. Regs., Part II. and the Staff Manual respectively. Title Pages will be prepared in manuscript.

Place	Date	Hour DAY	Summary of Events and Information	Remarks and references to Appendices
Ytres	19/11	Monday	Obtained 2 M.G. mountings for 109 M.G.C. all now complete for the offensive. 16 ph. o.2-4.5" Howr Owners but not yet arrived. Ordered huts from Corps Troop their meeting "Q" Euploral.	
	20/11	Tuesday	Attack this morning after week of past week a tire enquiries. We are not quite so unanimous. 18 ph. gun applied for M143 sent informed returned to-day. Water CarV demanded to 24/43. 31st Inf also received.	
	21/11	W/W	2/Cpl Hunt arrived from 5th Div. to relieve L/Cpl Speed who is to transferred to Inf.	
	22/11	Thurs	In office most of day. Saw Staff-Capt. Arty. I arranged early removal of guns at Lam. I received 400 pr Socks urgently required by 1st & 9th R.I.F. delivered at Stag Heap 2 am.	
	23/11	Friday	Rode with A.D.M.G in afternoon. Sent lorry to Q.P. for magazines urgently required by 109 Bde. received. also delivered 1006 Sim. Water to L/Cpl Quinn at Stag Heap.	
	24/11	Sat.	Went to Corps in morning to explain gun left in 1019 workshop by a Battery officer return of guns have ordered by Army Commander. Demanded various items discharged by Able Line	

2449 Wt. W14957/M90 750.000 1/16 J.B.C. & A. Forms/C.2118/12.

WAR DIARY or INTELLIGENCE SUMMARY

Army Form C. 2118.

Place	Date	Hour	Summary of Events and Information	Remarks and references to Appendices
Oteo	25/7 Sun.		Short morning in usual office routine. Lyon visited A.D.O.S. at Corps & 18th Left in Workshop. Several units demanding blankets urgently, none having been received from other Divisions for fortnight. Was able to collect from other Divisions only 1 RE Division called for return of all Special Stores demanded amongst	
	26/7 Mon.		Morning usual office work. Afternoon received intimation that more and Lucked up in readiness.	
	27/7 Tues.		Div W/Ds moved to Little Wood Stores, but owing to lack of accommodation there, moved office to Durnh at Bero. Men had to go under canvas as there is only the one hut there.	
Bero	28/7 Wed.		Visited H⁰ 2ⁿᵈ R.A. & infantry units with reference to forthcoming move.	
	29/7 Thurs.		Walked to Corps to try to get extra lorries for clearing Salvage & Ordnance Stores to Hartheal. Bee wined to new area, unable to move other t Bero and Office because of lorries being required for other work Estaffetti. Pioneers and E Companies R.E. transferred to 5th Division Stores etc & Bero had to leave Reserve.	
	30/7 Fri.		Moved office to Zevens. On arrival at new area found Division Stores behind moving back and later moved to Cohiet - to Heizz during night.	

Whealing Capt.
D.A.D.O.S. 34 Div

WAR DIARY / INTELLIGENCE SUMMARY

Army Form C. 2118.

DADOS 36th Division

Vol 24

Place	Date	Hour	Summary of Events and Information	Remarks and references to Appendices
Achiet le Petit	1/7 Saturday		Arrived at Achiet-le-Petit at 2 a.m. During morning moved back to old dump at Bus. Busy clearing trucks which were awaiting unloading at Achiet-le-Grand during remainder of day.	
Bus	2/7 Sunday		Visited Res. H.Q. and units, who were unsettled, and therefore had not been on drawing stores, which were sent out by lorries.	
	3/7 Monday		Walked to Pys H.Q. and units of 109 Bde.	
	4/7 Tuesday		Division again on the move so sent out stores to Lorries and was able to satisfy all demands for Lewis Guns and nearly all for Lone Pts.	
	5/7 Wed.		Had car and worked new area. Not satisfied with Dump Lorry vacated by 29 Div., but found Helmuth Dump at Nurlu. Store sent out to Bos by Lorries.	
Lone	6/7 Thurs		Stores moved to Heudecourt and my office to Lone. 29 Div Artillery attached for Ordnance.	
	7/7 Friday		By car to Amiens for I.P.	
	8/7 Saturday		Heavy column came into Lone, and as my lorries are not allowed on the roads, arranged with Light Railway outfit. Passed my Dump for transfer of stores from Herbal Europe to Light Railway at this point. Also sent by car 2 Lewis Guns and magazines from Advanced Gun Park.	

WAR DIARY or INTELLIGENCE SUMMARY

Army Form C. 2118.

(Erase heading not required.)

Instructions regarding War Diaries and Intelligence Summaries are contained in F. S. Regs., Part II. and the Staff Manual respectively. Title Pages will be prepared in manuscript.

Place	Date	Hour	Summary of Events and Information	Remarks and references to Appendices
Ord. 6. Gérard	9/1/17 Sunday		Visited A.D.O.S Corps & several units in morning. Office routine in afternoon	
	10/1/17 Monday		Moved my office to hut near Corps H.Q.S, by G.S wagon. Stores had to be taken by Light Railway to Dump. Harness of Hair Haitians found this method so not suitable & then took nearly 12 hours from time of leaving trucks on Broad Gauge to arrival at my Dump.	
	11/1/17 Tues.		Show notations removed, but some have a great amount of rack work to fuel up, in particular, to move the rest of Reserve Gun Boots from Bro to Clarke Lent out by Somus Gun Boots Bright to Bois Transport Lens	
	12/1/17 Wed.		Visited Corps & Dump in morning. Afternoon usual office routine. Our Corps returned to me for administration.	
	13/1/17 Thurs		Very busy all day with indents which, after the recent operations, are very heavy. Sent Reserve Store from Bro to Clarke & G.M. Butts to Gun Park.	
	14/1/17 Friday		Visited Corps Dépôts to discuss handing over French Stores to incoming Division.	
	15/1/17 Sat.		Engaged during morning and afternoon in making preparations for coming move. Packed up in evening ready to move off early following day.	

Army Form C. 2118.

WAR DIARY
or
INTELLIGENCE SUMMARY

(Erase heading not required.)

Instructions regarding War Diaries and Intelligence Summaries are contained in F. S. Regs., Part II. and the Staff Manual respectively. Title Pages will be prepared in manuscript.

Place	Date	Hour	Summary of Events and Information	Remarks and references to Appendices
Sonpt to Lucknow	16/1/17	Sunday	Move office and 1 B.O.R. stores to Lucknow, more everything nearly all day, owing to congestion of traffic on roads. At night, went back to supervise moving rest of dump from Paulu.	
Lucknow	17/1/17	Monday	107 B.O.C. W.D. unit stores left for Lucknow, but could get no further than Achenw. My car was also ordered up and I was compelled to put up for night in Achenw.	
"	18/1/17	Tuesday	The roads still impassable, and a mass of traffic held up, making it impossible to move either way.	
"	19/1/17	Wed.	Succeeded in reaching Lucknow, to find several units complaining of inability to obtain foodstuffs or make contact wherever Capt. Manson had been made for supply of Divisions, and some soonr returned.	
"	20/1/17	Thurs	Several trucks at Railhead awaiting clearance, and dump is not big enough to clear all stores being received especially as several units, not having settled in their area, have been unable to draw.	
"	21/1/17	Friday	Still more trucks arrived, and have now ample supplies of Boot, Clothing and Horseshoes to meet requirements of all Divisions. 108 Bde W.O. moved to Lucknow.	

Army Form C. 2118.

WAR DIARY
or
INTELLIGENCE SUMMARY

(Erase heading not required.)

Instructions regarding War Diaries and Intelligence Summaries are contained in F. S. Regs., Part II. and the Staff Manual respectively. Title Pages will be prepared in manuscript.

Place	Date	Hour	Summary of Events and Information	Remarks and references to Appendices
Lahore	22/12/17 Saturday		Visited Corps and I.O.R. Workshops to arrange his inspection Visited Corps & Field Kitchens which are generally in a bad state of repair after repeated moves and recent move to the Workshops are too far away to be convenient.	
"	23/12/17 Sunday		Spent day in inspecting, along with I.O.R. transport of several Battalions.	
"	24/12/17 Mon.		Went to Calais for purpose of getting from Exp. and Base Depôts more War mancoeuvre mules of the Base having any stock.	
"	25/12/17 Tues.		Usual office routine in morning. All offices closed as far as possible.	
"	26/12/17 Wed.		Owing to thaw scheme, was unable to clear Railhead. Reconsigned truck to new Railhead. Spent afternoon in office work. Reserve Stores truck up in loads and wagons for entrainment loading up on train one lorry sent to move dept Etaknu from 65's Division to new area.	
"	27/12/17 Thurs.		Several journeys made by lorries with stores to Railhead while stores where dumped. 107 Base M.T. moved to Corbie.	

WAR DIARY or INTELLIGENCE SUMMARY

Army Form C. 2118.

Place	Date	Hour	Summary of Events and Information	Remarks and references to Appendices
Lucknow	28th July		Offices moved from Lucknow to Carbu	
Carbu	29th July		Very little accommodation in the offices provided and had to get another room though this is inconvenient.	
"	30th July		Then the move very many orders in official capacity so Battery which has been detached temporarily is just getting on horses again	
"	31st July		It is considered advisable to move Dump to Carbu as this place will be more convenient when Horse Institution came into force, and so also never many of the Battalions Moves one Brigade to Carbu.	

Musgrove
Capt RA

WAR DIARY
or
INTELLIGENCE SUMMARY

Army Form C. 2118.

DADOS
36th Divn.

Place	Date	Hour	Summary of Events and Information	Remarks and references to Appendices
Corbie	1st June		Moved dumps of 108" and 109" Bdes. and Armourers Shops to Cachy.	
"	2nd "		Moved office to more convenient room nearer Div H.Q.s.	
"	3rd "		Artillery Dumps moved to Cachy.	
"	4th "		In company with the C.I.C.M. I inspected transport of 108th Bde.	
"	5th "		Saturday Usual office routine. Lt McClinton reported to me for instruction.	
"	6th "		Sunday Usual office routine. Visited Dumps at Cachy.	
"	7th "		Monday Moved office and stores to Harbonnières.	
Harbonnières	8th "		Tuesday Usual office routine. Brought fresh meat for Artillery locally, and delivered by car.	
"	9th "		Wed. Usual office routine. 107", 109" Bde Dumps moved to Cachy.	
"	10th "		Thurs. I visited new Dumps and arranged for Offices, Workshops &c.	

WAR DIARY
or
INTELLIGENCE SUMMARY

(Erase heading not required.)

Army Form C. 2118.

Place	Date	Hour	Summary of Events and Information	Remarks and references to Appendices
Shabanien	11/1/18	Fri.	1 ton Aeroplane Repair Stores etc drawn from Reserve. 1 car alluring has took of Gun Parts from Corps Troops Park. Truck Salvage Detach.	
	12/1/18	Sat.	Divil. H.Q. any office to move to Olazzy to-day but owing to then restrictions office gear had to be conveyed by G.S. wagon. Arrived at rail head & fixed up in an obviously temporary office at 5 p.m.	
	13/1/18	Sun.	Visited Dump at Olazzy spend work proceeding satisfactorily except difficulty in getting rations.	
	14/1/18	Mon.	Spent the day in office continued journey to Olazzy when owing to delayed evacuation of French Troops accomodation is very limited & office is opened temporally in garage shared with O.R.E. to have a place with us near Dump which will be ready in a week or ten	
	15/1/18	Tues.	Thaw restrictions again in force markhead will have to be closed by H.T. for a few days. Several tons of general area stores etc drawn from Corps Troops Park by G.S. wagon - Shrubs, Storm, Brazier, Hot Food Containers, for "Q" distribution.	

WAR DIARY
INTELLIGENCE SUMMARY

Army Form C. 2118.

(Erase heading not required.)

Place	Date	Hour	Summary of Events and Information	Remarks and references to Appendices
Oussy	16/4/18	Wed.	Work of drawing several tow gun Raiders by H.T. taken up whole day. Moved office writer in g. branch most of day. Gun Boots carried to Bris HQs as per instructions from "Q".	
	17/4/18	Thurs.	Visit Amiens to purchase for G.S.O.1	
	18/4/18	Fri.	Further 1000 pra Gum Boots Thigh drawn from C.I. Stum making 3500 pr. received to date. A.A.G. Corps called in morning	
	19/4/18	Sat.	Wires for Lewis Gun for m.E.T. Also 1 Vickers Gun for 107 M.G. Coy.	
	20/4/18	Sun.	266 Machine Gun Coy joined Division but no incidents reported. Demanded 500 Hopper fans.	
	21/4/18	Mon.	Usual office routine	
	22/4/18	Tues.	To Gun Park at Albert. O.I.O.m. 2 Lorries to Harbonniers to clear stores of Camp Commandants Armourils.	

M6945. Wt. W11422/M1169. 35,000 12/16 D.D.&L. Forms/C/2118/14.

WAR DIARY
or
INTELLIGENCE SUMMARY.
(Erase heading not required.)

Army Form C. 2118.

Instructions regarding War Diaries and Intelligence Summaries are contained in F. S. Regs., Part II. and the Staff Manual respectively. Title pages will be prepared in manuscript.

Place	Date	Hour	Summary of Events and Information	Remarks and references to Appendices
Alex	2/3		Naval office routine	
	14th	Thurs	Received Lewis Guns for 1st R.N.B.	
	15th	Frid	Instructed No 1 Heavy R.M.M. to fit on rail any vehicles ready. Demanded 1800 Water Tins	
	16th	Sat	Naval office routine	
	17th	Sun	Naval office routine	
	18th	Mon	Cpl MacKayie went on leave. Duties taken over by Cpl Whittaker	
	19th	Tues	Two one vehicles arrived at Railhead. Work advised to clear	
	20th	Wed	Half a dozen vehicles damaged by French & Greeks collecting stored up earth. I.O.C. Vulcatches [?]	

A6915 Wt.W14422/M1160 35,000 12/16 D.D. & L. Forms/C./2118/14.

WAR DIARY
INTELLIGENCE SUMMARY.
(Erase heading not required.)

Army Form C. 2118.

Place	Date	Hour	Summary of Events and Information	Remarks and references to Appendices
Albert	27/11		Wet. made necessary arrangements. Sure men from 128 Bde reported for duty. they are to relieve 2 Ordnance men required by Corps for re-organisation of Divisions.	
	28th		ADOS visited office and dump and gave instructions on re-organisation and procedure to be taken in returning stores to Base.	

W.W. Dusling
Lt
ADADOS
36 Division

NANTS 76 Vol 26

WAR DIARY
or
INTELLIGENCE SUMMARY
(Erase heading not required.)

Army Form C. 2118.

Place	Date	Hour	Summary of Events and Information	Remarks and references to Appendices
Alley	1.1.18 Friday		Went to Ham to buy Chain required by armourer for use in Modification of Elevating Gear for Vickers Gun but could not get what was required. Demanded 1000 Pillowers.	
	2.2.18 Saty		Went by car to Amiens and was able to get chain.	
	3.3.18 Sun		All available men engaged in building up Lorry which will be required for taking in and storing mobilization stores to be handed in by Battalions being disbanded.	
	4.4.18 Mon		Went to Ham to purchase building supplements for Area Commandant – Antwerp. Mobilization stores of 8/9 R.I.R. taken in.	
	5.5.18 Tues		Sent lorry to Albert to draw 1 Lewis Gun for 8/9 R.I.R. and other Vickers & Lewis Gun Parts	

WAR DIARY
or
INTELLIGENCE SUMMARY.
(Erase heading not required.)

Army Form C. 2118.

Instructions regarding War Diaries and Intelligence Summaries are contained in F. S. Regs., Part II, and the Staff Manual respectively. Title pages will be prepared in manuscript.

Place	Date	Hour	Summary of Events and Information	Remarks and references to Appendices
Alloa	6.2.18 Wed		Machine gun store of 10' Pl. Machine Gun training handed in.	
"	7.2.18 Thur		Machine gun store of 11' Pl. machine gun training handed in.	
"	8.2.18 Friday		A further consignment of stores from 10' Pl. having the stores were received. These stores having been left at Burntisland. Stores beginning to arrive for 1st and 2nd Pl. musketry training. Received by consignment of Blanks &S.	
"	9.2.18 Sat		Making progress in improvement of Camp, but could do with more material than I can obtain from R.E.s to complete to satisfaction.	
"	10.2.18 Mon		Usual routine	
"	11.2.18 Tues		Armourers busily engaged in putting into good order Lewis Guns returned by disbanded Battalions. Shelter attempted Court of Enquiry into Tram Accident at Ham	
"	13.2.18 Wed		Went to Ainero by car to make several local Purchases	

Army Form C. 2118.

WAR DIARY
or
INTELLIGENCE SUMMARY.
(Erase heading not required.)

Instructions regarding War Diaries and Intelligence Summaries are contained in F.S. Regs., Part II. and the Staff Manual respectively. Title pages will be prepared in manuscript.

Place	Date	Hour	Summary of Events and Information	Remarks and references to Appendices
Ollezy	14.2.18	Thurs	Demanded at Lewis Guns for Division from Fifth Army Gun Park. Lt. Waite Army Inspector of Armourers inspected Armourer's Workshop.	
"	15.2.18	Fri.	Interviewed A.A. & Q.M.G. with reference to new form for Monthly Return of Salvage to be issued by Units and also a Monthly Return to be rendered by Salvage. This new scheme was adopted and will come into force forthwith.	
"	16.2.18	Sat.	Returned to O.C. Echo Trench 27 also at Bohadilly returned to one by Artillery Units and drew 10 Vickers A.A. Posts Mountings for 266 M.G. Coy. Sent to Fifth Army Gun Park the Lewis Guns and accessories handed in by disbanded Units.	
"	17.2.18	Sun.	Issued to each Inf. Bde. H.Q. 350 Hopkin Sans Rifle mobilization stores of disbanded Battalions in cases and packages.	

A6945 Wt. W14422/M160 35,000 12/16 D.D. & L. Forms/C./2118/14.

WAR DIARY
INTELLIGENCE SUMMARY

Army Form C. 2118.

(Erase heading not required.)

Place	Date	Hour	Summary of Events and Information	Remarks and references to Appendices
Olley	18.2.18	Morn	Returned to Railhead for despatch to Base all stores rendered surplus by re-organization. Sent lorry to Corps Troops for 350 Petrol Tins.	
"	19.2.18	Noon	Three of my lorries collected Mobilization Stores of 11/53 R.I.R. Stores of 10th & 11th R.I.R. sent in by unit. Collected from 5th Army Gun Park 29 Lewis Guns for R.P. Defence in Division. Vehicles collected yesterday thoroughly cleaned and prepared for issue.	
"	20.2.18	Aft	Drew Lewis Stores from Gun Park no 3, including Lewis Guns for 2 H.Q. Irish Fusiliers.	
"	21.2.18	Morn	Normal routine.	

WAR DIARY
or
INTELLIGENCE SUMMARY.

(Erase heading not required.)

Army Form C. 2118.

Instructions regarding War Diaries and Intelligence Summaries are contained in F. S. Regs., Part II. and the Staff Manual respectively. Title pages will be prepared in manuscript.

Place	Date	Hour	Summary of Events and Information	Remarks and references to Appendices
Villers	22/12	Fri	Owing to thaw scheme being in force, was unable to clear to Railhead several sacks of worn-out clothing, shirts, shoes, sheets & returned by disbanded Units. D.D.O.S. Fifth Army rerouted Dump.	
"	23rd	Sat	Capt. L.C. Mackenzie MC returned from leave and took over duties from Lt. Woolstar.	
			Returned to Railhead, mobilisation stories of "M", "L", "H", "E", Battalions. R.Ps. all having to be carried in G.S. Wagons owing to thaw restrictions.	
	24th	Sun	Usual office routine.	
	25th	Mon	Returned to Gun Park no 5. The Lewis Guns of the Last 4 Battalions disbanded.	

A6915 Wt. W14422/M1160 35,000 12/16 D.D.& L. Forms/C./2118/14.

Army Form C. 2118.

WAR DIARY
or
INTELLIGENCE SUMMARY.
(Erase heading not required.)

Instructions regarding War Diaries and Intelligence Summaries are contained in F. S. Regs., Part II. and the Staff Manual respectively. Title pages will be prepared in manuscript.

Place	Date	Hour	Summary of Events and Information	Remarks and references to Appendices
Ollay	26th Tuesday Monday		Recd. H.Q. Patrol Line from XVIII Corps Troops. All these require a thorough cleaning and necessitate my getting more labour from A.P.L. Many indents serving over due in part to new order whereby all details indents outstanding more than 6 months are automatically cancelled and fresh indent necessary unless stock has now no need of stores.	
"	27th Wed. Tues.		Sent lorry to Gun Park to draw 5 Hotchkiss L.G.s and a further 16 Lewis Guns for use as anti-aircraft defence. Visit . . . . labour Troops	
"	28th Thurs. Wed		Visited Italian Labour Coy, and inspected transport re– turned by discharged units. I notice that an increasing proportion of indents are being signed by officers other than C.O.	

[signature] Lt. Col. [signature]

WAR DIARY or INTELLIGENCE SUMMARY

Army Form C. 2118.

36th Divn.

Place	Date	Hour	Summary of Events and Information	Remarks and references to Appendices
Mlley	1st	Orders	All Gun Stores are now being drawn from Gun Park at M.S. and I have transferred all items still outstanding from Gun Park no.1 to new Park. The Machine Gun Coys. from today are combined to form one complete unit to be known as 36 Bn M.G.Cy. and all outstanding returns of the old Coys are now cancelled. Visits 1st R. In. Fus. 2 R. In. Rifles 9th R. Ir. Fus. 12 R In Rifles & R. Innis. Fus. units re. D.A.Q.M.G. very few stores being held in Store by any unit	
	2nd	Sunday	Usual routine	
	3rd		Every Drew all new pattern anti-aircraft mountings for Lewis Guns inspected by G.O.C. Division	
	4th	May	Captain C.A. Mackenzie left for course of instruction	

WAR DIARY
INTELLIGENCE SUMMARY
(Erase heading not required.)

Army Form C. 2118.

Instructions regarding War Diaries and Intelligence Summaries are contained in F. S. Regs., Part II. and the Staff Manual respectively. Title pages will be prepared in manuscript.

Place	Date	Hour	Summary of Events and Information	Remarks and references to Appendices
Abbey	4/3 Monday		No 14 Clearance Dypt. Major Harmer taking over the duties during his absence. 200 Head Lines drawn from Corps Troops. 136 Italian Labour Coy arrived	
"	5/3 Tues		Move 1st & 102nd Entrenching Battalions to 5th Army Troops	
"	6/3 Wed		Moved 66" Italian Labour Coy to 3rd Corps Troops	
"	7/3 Thur		Received 1 Lewis Gun for 4th H.Schnichalling Tractors and 1 Hotchkiss Gun for Div. Supply Column. Also drew from Corps Troops 1 Perrocepe no 5.	
"	8/3 Friday		Received another consignment of Timber and building material for building accommodation for men. 15" D.L.R. complained of inability to obtain	

Army Form C. 2118.

WAR DIARY
or
INTELLIGENCE SUMMARY.
(Erase heading not required.)

Instructions regarding War Diaries and Intelligence Summaries are contained in F. S. Regs., Part II. and the Staff Manual respectively. Title pages will be prepared in manuscript.

Place	Date	Hour	Summary of Events and Information	Remarks and references to Appendices
Allipp	Aug 8th		Capt Kering Rifle Brigade but on investigation found not was at fault.	
"	Sat 9th	9/15	Captain Coles MC Took over duties as D.A.D.O.S.	
"	Sun 10th		None routine	
"	Mon 11th	3/15	188 Italian Labour Coy arrived	
"	Tues 12th		426 shares of Gum Boots Thigh divided by 108" Bde H.Q. and sent there by 109 Bde H.Q.	
"	Wed 13th		Conductor Brennan visited and took out stores to 186 and 188 Italian Labour Coys. Issued Water Tins to east Infantry Bde. Received 1 Lewis Gun for 1 R.I.R.	

A6945. Wt. W14422/M1160 35,000 12/16 D.D.&L. Forms/C/2118/14.

Army Form C. 2118.

WAR DIARY
or
INTELLIGENCE SUMMARY.
(Erase heading not required.)

Instructions regarding War Diaries and Intelligence Summaries are contained in F. S. Regs., Part II. and the Staff Manual respectively. Title pages will be prepared in manuscript.

Place	Date	Hour	Summary of Events and Information	Remarks and references to Appendices
Alley	14/3 Thurs		Received 10 Anti-Aircraft Mountings Lewis Guns and 10 Anti-Aircraft Vickers Mountings with Adapters for Lewis Guns.	
"	15/3 Friday		Sent Lorry to Gun Park no 5 to draw 1 Patt 08/15 German Machine Gun, which is to be held for instructional purposes by Div Machine Gun Battalion for 1 month.	
"	16/3 Sat		Under Army instructions, all armourers are now to be in Divisional Workshop, which is to be formed into two departments, one for inspecting arms, bicycles &c, and one for repairs. All Machine Guns are to periodically thoroughly inspected and tested.	

WAR DIARY or INTELLIGENCE SUMMARY

Army Form C. 2118.

Place	Date	Hour	Summary of Events and Information	Remarks and references to Appendices
Villagio	17/5 Sun.		Supply Collection 1100 fuchile and 1000 fins Taverna Cdo di Frenzi Caspo Croopio	
	18/5 Mon		3 Officers Mess Carts brought up by 26 M.C. Batt'n were at once allowed 1 per Battalion instead of 1 per Coy.	
	19/5 Tues		All ammuno in shof puts on waterproofs	
	20/5 Wed		Line to help clearing of Livine. Received 50 sets of tent batteries for Motion Platoon. Coys and sent them to Place with by lorries. Also collected from Coys Trucks of further 508 Jackets S.D. 200 Fustenana and 800 fins Pattees	
	21/5 Thurs		Only a few scouts made, as all Battalions transport fetch up German made their offensive. Capt C.A. Mackenzie R.E. against from course of instruction in ammunition. Two lorries returned to supply Column under Cpl unstructions and remaining two in use	

A6945 Wt. W14727/M160 35,000 12/16 D.D. & L. Forms/C/2118/14.

WAR DIARY
or
INTELLIGENCE SUMMARY.
(Erase heading not required.)

Army Form C. 2118.

Place	Date	Hour	Summary of Events and Information	Remarks and references to Appendices
Olezy	21/3		By Corps Commanders and an emergency I was unable to move back a great amount of reserve stores	
Francile	22/3		Having moved office dumps anti-gas appliances and important stores to trucks but balance shifts here also were clothing had to be abandoned, information to bring back train for any second trip as we left OLEZY at 10.45 A.M. & the enemy was through ARTEMPS	
			Allocal 20 Lewis guns & 8 Vickers from O.P.	
Beaulieu	22/3		Moved to Beaulieu & rested	
Eurebigy	22/3		Moved to Eurebigy. Sent advanced billets devised for Lova- had to be hee Bill writes for to stop.	
"	23/3		Was able to make rooms to Battalions of necessary equipment, rifles, box respirators ac	
Gricourt	23/3		Moved to Gricourt. Made none of my Lorries etc. unpacked. Made issues of clothing to such of the troops as were in the neighbourhood.	

Army Form C. 2118.

WAR DIARY
or
INTELLIGENCE SUMMARY.
(Erase heading not required.)

Instructions regarding War Diaries and Intelligence Summaries are contained in F. S. Regs., Part II. and the Staff Manual respectively. Title pages will be prepared in manuscript.

Place	Date	Hour	Summary of Events and Information	Remarks and references to Appendices
Chemont	2/12	Wed	Began work this time to Chemont. Issued every thing I had on the stores to 119. Bde.	
Containe	18/12	Thur	Moved to Containe	
Wally	19/12	Fri	Moved to Wally	
Gomarcho	20/12	Sat	Moved to Gomarcho	
	21/12	Sunday	Went up dumps for 108, 109 Bdes. Received consignment of blankets from Le Trefort and sent lorries to Abbeville for various other stores urgently required.	

Ernest Capp
Capt
O/C Divnammn

A6945 Wt. W14422/M1160. 35,000 12/16 D.D. & L. Forms/C/2118/14.

WAR DIARY
or
INTELLIGENCE SUMMARY.
(Erase heading not required.)

Army Form C. 2118.

Dadps
36th Divn
Vol 28

Place	Date	Hour	Summary of Events and Information	Remarks and references to Appendices
Gonnades	1/10	Monday	Got available lorries out to various units received consignment of blankets and shirts ground.	
	2/10	Tuesday	Demanded 90 lorries and 5th Vickers Guns to complete Division. Fifteen tons of service dress belts and under clothing arrived. In view of move and urgency in refitting division, this clothing was loaded up on lorries and sent by road instead of re-consigning to Div. Duty in running in old area Left Staff arr. Div. Arty at Poza.	
Pockheb	4/10	Thursday	Both M.G. 10/ D.O.R. moved to new area. Office and part of dump opened at Pockheb near International Corner.	

WAR DIARY
or
INTELLIGENCE SUMMARY.

(Erase heading not required.)

Army Form C. 2118.

Place	Date	Hour	Summary of Events and Information	Remarks and references to Appendices
Pollock	5th May		Officer arrived at Tom Chic Camp and remainder of troops arrived at Pollock. By car to Calais taking a couple of lorries where I obtained eight rifles, flannelette, bayonets & lubricating steel planks &c. all of which are most urgently required.	
Tom Chic	6th May		Very busy day with contents received by lorries & 2 Vickers Guns. Also issued for another 6500 rounds and 100 fm Jackets to left divisions, the old clothing discarded to be washed, disinfected and re-issued.	
	7th May		Sent out clothing and machine guns to 108 Bn who have explained that they cannot get stores from Ordnance, though none of the men have visited the Camp. On the other hand, the 109 Bde are well satisfied with the early replies to our requisitions.	

WAR DIARY
or
INTELLIGENCE SUMMARY.

(Erase heading not required.)

Army Form C. 2118.

Place	Date	Hour	Summary of Events and Information	Remarks and references to Appendices
Siege Camp	8th	Monday	Moved office and dump to Siege Camp. Received 69 Lewis Guns and 1408 magazines.	
"	9th	Tues	I visited all Infantry Battalions.	
"	10th	Wed	Demanded 47 Lewis Guns for the M.G. Bn. 108" Bde and 1 Coy of M.G. Bn. to move to Welcorts. I am taking over at dump any extra Lewis Guns by	
"	11th	Thurs	Received 7 Stokes Mortars	
"	12th	Fri	Received 17 Lewis Guns demanded for M.G. Bn. and delivered it to company lying at Welcorts. Received to 183rd H.Q. Received Trench Lead and balance to be issued available.	
Siege Camp	13th	Satdy	Moved office to Van Hone Farm and Dump to International Corner. Seven Armourers surplus to establishment by re-organization of Divison sent to Base. Received 20 Elephant R.R. Lights for Machine Guns	

WAR DIARY
or
INTELLIGENCE SUMMARY.

(Erase heading not required.)

Army Form C. 2118.

Instructions regarding War Diaries and Intelligence Summaries are contained in F. S. Regs., Part II. and the Staff Manual respectively. Title pages will be prepared in manuscript.

Place	Date	Hour	Summary of Events and Information	Remarks and references to Appendices
Dragon Camp	14/2	Cont	2/Lt Allen, who joined for duty on 1st inst. moved to Corps Troops. Received 5 Stokes Mortars and several vehicles.	
Dragon Camp	15/2	Morn	March to camp vacated by 1.R.B. 11 v. 16 O.P.W.R.	
"	16/2	Eve	Received truck of bath stores for sec duty and used 9 Corps troops to clear.	
"	17/2	Wed	Sent men to Proven without to receive certain items of winter clothing which on return we likely to be small, as most of this clothing has been lost.	
"	18/2	Thurs	Dump moved into same camp as office. Collected 10 Principee no 31 and 1 Part M/G formed from Corps Troops Coll. the out of Lock Sect. left at camp taken over by 109 Fld Ambulance. Hour commenced sent	
"	19/2	Friday	to reconnaissance across of 108 Bde, who have new rejoined the Division.	
"	20/21 Sat		Demanded 16 Lewis Guns for 11 R.I.R.	
"	21/2 Sun		Usual routine. All carriers now working in Div Sch.	

Army Form C. 2118.

WAR DIARY
or
INTELLIGENCE SUMMARY.
(Erase heading not required.)

Instructions regarding War Diaries and Intelligence Summaries are contained in F. S. Regs., Part II. and the Staff Manual respectively. Title pages will be prepared in manuscript.

Place	Date	Hour	Summary of Events and Information	Remarks and references to Appendices
Dragon Camp	21st Mon		Recommended 4 Lewis Guns for 9" R.I.F. and received 12 for 18" R.I.F.	
"	22nd Tues		Usual office routine	
"	23rd Wed		Div Artillery ordered Sent lorry to 9" O.T. for lamps. Legs and harness for raft.	
"	24th Thurs		One lorry went to Gun Park Whatton to pick up guns and deliver same to 4"th Workshops, also to Trail London Carriage to 162nd & 286th R.F.A. I visited Calais in order to obtain several important small items.	
"	25th Fri		Attended conference of Staff Officers called to consider suggestions for proposed reduction of unnecessary mobilization stores.	
Calais	26th Sat		Usual office and dump to Prevent	
"	27th Sun		was able to make only a few repairs, several went wrong on the march	

Army Form C. 2118.

WAR DIARY
or
INTELLIGENCE SUMMARY.
(Erase heading not required.)

Place	Date	Hour	Summary of Events and Information	Remarks and references to Appendices
La Louie	29th	Morn	Moved office to La Louie Chateau.	
	30th		Camps congested with others, accomodation shift due to duplication of several demands by Base.	

Wm Tapp
Lt Col
a/c Director

D.A.D.O.S.
36th Division
Vol VIV

WAR DIARY
or
INTELLIGENCE SUMMARY.
(Erase heading not required.)

Army Form C. 2118.

Place	Date	Hour	Summary of Events and Information	Remarks and references to Appendices
La Panne	1/12 Wed		Usual routine. Hastened Baga Tool Shoemakers none of which has been received yet, though nearly all were in need of them.	
"	2/12 Thur		Went to Gun Park at Wharton by car to show a Bosch Mechanism	
"	3/12 Frid		Usual routine	
"	4/12 Sat		Dumps not able to cope with stores accumulating owing to Base having duplicated demands	
"	5/12 Sun		Usual routine	
"	6/12 Mon		Usual routine	
"	7/12 Tues		Visited Railhead to arrange clearance of new stores not required. Demanded 18 pr gun for	
"	8/12 Wed		Visited dump. Usual routine	
"	9/12 Thurs		To Calais by car to investigate numerous duplications of Base stores demanded, and to make	

WAR DIARY or INTELLIGENCE SUMMARY

Army Form C. 2118.

(Erase heading not required.)

Instructions regarding War Diaries and Intelligence Summaries are contained in F. S. Regs., Part II. and the Staff Manual respectively. Title pages will be prepared in manuscript.

Place	Date	Hour	Summary of Events and Information	Remarks and references to Appendices
Caythorpe Kyalami Xxxx	9/12 Thurs(day)		several local funerals. Moved office to Caythorpe	
	10/12 Fri		Visited dumps. Sent lorry to Whatton to fetch	
	11/12 Sat		Left refs. & 18th gun and to take them on to 1 O.P. Wenbeloye	
	12/12 Sat		Issued 8 Hob. Pivoters to 11. G. Battalion and 5 Periscopes to Div. Arty. The Brown commenced work as Divisional Shoemaker	
	13/12 Sun		Demanded 1 Stokes Mortar to replace 1 of 10/77/23 destroyed by shell fire.	
	13/12 Mon		Visited dump in morning; afternoon usual routine.	
	14/12 Tues		By car to Eton Park to settle several questions which has arisen in particular the supply of N. C. O's. Returned four of men attached to their units.	

Army Form C. 2118.

WAR DIARY
or
INTELLIGENCE SUMMARY.
(Erase heading not required.)

Instructions regarding War Diaries and Intelligence Summaries are contained in F.S. Regs., Part II. and the Staff Manual respectively. Title pages will be prepared in manuscript.

Place	Date	Hour	Summary of Events and Information	Remarks and references to Appendices
Couture	15th Wed		Visited dump and Div. H.Q. in morning. In afternoon to A.D.D.S. Received 1 Pistoning Machine for Vickers Gun on approval.	
Rebeng	16th Thurs		Visited to dump and Div. H.Q.	
	17th Friday		Held an A.D.O.S. and unofficial dump.	
	18th Sat		Usual routine.	
	19th Sun		Attended conference of DADOS at Corps to discuss new scheme of weekly issues of ration items to units and which is to allow receipt of antiservicable articles.	
	20th Mon		Went to Calais by car.	
	21st Tues		Visited several units including Machine Gun Battalion, and Battalions of 107 Inf Bde. none of whom have any complaints to make	

A6945 Wt.W1422/M1160 35,000 12/16 D.D.&L. Forms/C./2118/14.

WAR DIARY
or
INTELLIGENCE SUMMARY

Army Form C. 2118.

(Erase heading not required.)

Place	Date	Hour	Summary of Events and Information	Remarks and references to Appendices
Dragoon Camp	22/2 Wed		Marced office to Dragon Camp. Recconnoitred Lewis	
	23/2 Thurs		Guns to complete Batteries to Scale "B". Major Book of Second Army School of Sniping Division and after going onto Stabilus in visited the new Sniper Rifle issued 25 to each Battalion	
	24/2 Friday		Visited P.G. Battalion Lt. Lewis R.Lewis Lts attached to me for instruction in Ordnance Duties	
	25/2 Sat		Visited Dump and A.D.O.S Reserve Lewis. From 1st Division to Scale D.	
	26/2 Sun		Sent lorry to Gun Park to draw Lewis Guns to complete Division to Scale E.	
	27/2 Mon		Usual routine.	
	28/2 Tues		Visited Dump and A.D.O.S office.	
	29/2 Wed		Visited dump, usual routine.	

Army Form C. 2118.

WAR DIARY
or
INTELLIGENCE SUMMARY.
(Erase heading not required.)

Place	Date	Hour	Summary of Events and Information	Remarks and references to Appendices
Bryan Camp	20/3	Thurs	Went by car to Ludwing to arrange removal of reserve dumps. Brig there.	
	27/2	Friday	Usual routine; checked fresh evidents for Bicycles called for under GRO #109).	

Wheeler
Capt
06 Division

WAR DIARY or INTELLIGENCE SUMMARY

Army Form C. 2118.

D.A.D.O.S. 36th Division.

Place	Date	Hour	Summary of Events and Information	Remarks and references to Appendices
Dragon Camp	1st Sat		Went to Calais by car to make several local purchases.	
	2nd Sun		Visited dump's, council Hons Bill Commandant (Equidale Station) to Machine Gun Battalion.	
Couthove	3rd Mon		Office moved to Couthove Chateau.	
	4th Tues		Usual routine. Visited Rifle Grenade Discharger Course to Battalions.	
	5th Wed		Visited ADOS II Corps. write of 108th Inf. Bde. and dumps.	
	6th Thurs		Visited dumps.	
	7th Frid		Went to St Omer to make several local purchases. The chief item being paints for which all units are asking so that they may ever haul and re-paint vehicles now they are out of line. Also went to Divisional Dump at Arobrucq.	

WAR DIARY
INTELLIGENCE SUMMARY
(Erase heading not required.)

Army Form C. 2118.

Place	Date	Hour	Summary of Events and Information	Remarks and references to Appendices
Carthose	8th	Sat	Returned to Army Troops at Rombies. 4th Hacks carrying Water Line. Armourers sent out to 108 & 109 Bties to overhaul and inspect arms of Batteries.	
"	9th	Sun	Visited Pump, which is working satisfactorily. Several men being sick. Armourer sent to inspect arms of 107 Bte.	
"	10th	Mon	Visited dump and M.T. Coy, from whom I borrowed spare drivers to replace sick men.	
"	11th	Tue	Went by car to Auberny. Two of my lorries reported there to remove Divisional Dump.	
"	12th	Wed	Two more lorries sent to Auberny to bring back the balance of Divisional Dump.	
"	13th	Thur	Visited dump; usual routine.	
"	14th	Friday	Visited dump and 12" R.L.R.	
"	15th	Sat	Pte J. Evans & G. Everett joined for duty from Havre.	

WAR DIARY
or
INTELLIGENCE SUMMARY.
(Erase heading not required.)

Army Form C. 2118.

Place	Date	Hour	Summary of Events and Information	Remarks and references to Appendices
Couture	16th Sun		Received Vickers Gun to replace one unserviceable.	
"	17th Mon		Pte. Dove and Hippli to Havre for tour of home service. Received Pte. R. Clifford Horne with Lewis Gunner	
"	18th Tues		for trial. Usual daily routine.	
"	19th Wed		Visited Dumps and 15th R.I.R.	
"	20th Thurs		Went by car to Calais	
"	21st Fri		Visited Dumps, usual routine	
"	22nd Sat		Received Limber Wagons for 15" & 16" R.I.R.	
"	23rd Sun		Demanded Lewis Guns to complete Battalions to scale G.	
"	24th Mon		Received Limber Wagon for 2nd R. Innis Fus and Telephone Wagon for Signals.	
"	25th Tues		Demanded from Base 6000 Rds Browero Shot for Baths. Received from Corps Troops 500 Lago Nose Juli for trial.	

Army Form C. 2118.

WAR DIARY
or
INTELLIGENCE SUMMARY.
(Erase heading not required.)

Place	Date	Hour	Summary of Events and Information	Remarks and references to Appendices
Carthona	16/2/18		16 BIR complained of shabbiness and disreputable appearance of washed Lewis Guns received after scavanging samples I considered their complaint perfectly justified. This was also pointed out from Bde fault in issued that being received from Bde showmen shown compares unfavourably with those issued in Battalion workshops.	
"	17/2/18	Morn	Collected 65 Lewis Guns as first lot of 95 required to complete Division in Scale G.	
"	18/2/18	Morn	Collected another 65 Lewis Guns from Gun Park	
"	19/2/18	Morn	Collected 65 Lewis Guns to complete Division	
"	20/2/18	Morn	None received	

(Signed) ?
Major
DADOS
36 Division

SADOT
36° Div.   Vol VII

Army Form C. 2118.

WAR DIARY
or
INTELLIGENCE SUMMARY.
(Erase heading not required.)

Place	Date	Hour	Summary of Events and Information	Remarks and references to Appendices
Couture Ret.	1/7/18 Mon		Divisional Horse Show and so far as possible, a holiday throughout the Division.	
"	2/7/18 Tues		Moved part of dump to Caool.	
"	3/7/18 Wed		Rest of dump, armourers shop and office moved Going to Caool.	
Caool	4/7/18 Thurs		Usual routine.	
"	5/7/18 Friday		Two lorries sent to Guitham to clear 8 tons of general stores and oil bicycles. One lorry to Lumbres to fetch up French shelters and tents which were sent out to various units. Wires for Stramba Horns sent to Bns. Baths for new sector.	
"	6/7/18 Sat.		Demanded Stokes barrel to replace one destroyed by premature. Moved office to Rue de St Omer.	
"	7/7/18 Sun		Lorry sent to Reserve Army Troops at Lumbres for further allotment of tents. Wired for Vickers Gun for M.G. Batt. for training personnel out of line.	

Army Form C. 2118.

WAR DIARY
or
INTELLIGENCE SUMMARY.
(Erase heading not required.)

Instructions regarding War Diaries and Intelligence Summaries are contained in F. S. Regs., Part II. and the Staff Manual respectively. Title pages will be prepared in manuscript.

Place	Date	Hour	Summary of Events and Information	Remarks and references to Appendices
Capel	8/4/18	Mon	Two lorries sent out to Artillery with tents and Trench shelter. Bde M.O's took out all available stores to work.	
"	9/4/18	Tues	Moved office to Terdeghem and dump to St Silvestre Cappel. Demanded by wire Vermorel Sprays, Vacuum Bulbs & and Buckets Latrine for new area.	
Terdeghem	10/4/18	Wed	Went by car to Millam.	
"	11/4/18	Thurs	Visited dump and railhead.	
"	12/4/18	Friday	Usual routine	
"	13/4/18	Sat.	Visited dump. Sent lorries to Proven to fetch 4ft Sub. Beds for Newton Mortars left there, but no trace of them could be found.	
"	14/4/18	Sun.	Went to Proven by car and found Sub. Beds had been taken into use by another Division. Wired for Sub. Bases for Bomb & Potato Dumps	

Army Form C. 2118.

WAR DIARY
or
INTELLIGENCE SUMMARY.
(Erase heading not required.)

Instructions regarding War Diaries and Intelligence Summaries are contained in F. S. Regs., Part II. and the Staff Manual respectively. Title pages will be prepared in manuscript.

Place	Date	Hour	Summary of Events and Information	Remarks and references to Appendices
Terdeghem	15th Mon.		I have opened Shoemaker's Shop to do repairs for any units not having a shoemaker, and two men for Employment Coy commenced work today.	
"	16th Tues		Sent lorry to + Corps Troops to draw 11 Tents and 55 Shelters. Chained to 110 Battery R.F.A 11 Tents and 30 Shelters. Magazine received with lot 8 Lewis Guns for Infantry Battalions sent to Audruicq for storage until such time as we have transport available for carriage.	
"	17th Wed		Went to Vendrouve to obtain Aerial Signalling Apparatus. Issued 10 Tents and 55 Shelters to 109 Bde.	
"	18th Thurs		Usual routine	
"	19th Fri		Visited Corps, Demanded and sent up to 108 Sge Bde 16 Lewis Guns to complete Batteries	
"	20th Sat		Demanded 16 Lewis Guns to complete 6 Lewis Guns of Artillery to scale of 4 per gun, and 6 Lewis Guns for Hd Corps R.E. to complete to same scale.	

Army Form C. 2118.

WAR DIARY
or
INTELLIGENCE SUMMARY.
(Erase heading not required.)

Instructions regarding War Diaries and Intelligence Summaries are contained in F. S. Regs., Part II. and the Staff Manual respectively. Title pages will be prepared in manuscript.

Place	Date	Hour	Summary of Events and Information	Remarks and references to Appendices
Tadworth	21/10 Sun		Church service	
"	22/10 Mon		Received 8 Army Boards for Divisional Artillery	
"	23/10 Tues		Received 16 Lewis Guns for Artillery and 100 Latrine Buckets for Divisional Area	
"	24/10 Wed		Attended conference of D.A.D's O.S. held at office of R.D.O.S. & Corps. Sent lorry to X Corps Troops to collect 20 French Shelters for issue to 109 Inf. Bde.	
"	25/10 Thurs		Usual routine. Inspected QM Store of 107 Bde.	
"	26/10 Friday		Went by car to Boulogne where I made arrangements for an Ordnance representative to be at Etaples when to attend to Div. Kingston Coy. Received 3 Lewis Guns to complete R.E. Companies.	
"	27/10 Sat		Lay sick in bed after inoculation.	
"	28/10 Sun			
"	29/10 Mon		Sent lorry to X Corps Troops for Tents, Shelters.	
"	30/10 Tues		Visited units of 107 and 108 Inf. Bdes. Lorry collected 250 combination anti-gas suits for	

WAR DIARY
or
INTELLIGENCE SUMMARY.
(Erase heading not required.)

Army Form C. 2118.

Place	Date	Hour	Summary of Events and Information	Remarks and references to Appendices
Longpré	27/10/16		Trial by Artillery Wirel. Sig. car to Surplus Personnel Camp at Longpré. Lorry sent to this Camp with stores	

Mauren
Major
GSO 1
36' Division

Army Form C. 2118.

DADOS
36th Div.

WAR DIARY
INTELLIGENCE SUMMARY.
(Erase heading not required.)

Place	Date	Hour	Summary of Events and Information	Remarks and references to Appendices
Tealightsw	1/8/18 Thurs		Usual routine. Visited Dumps	
"	2/8/18 Fri.		Visited Dumps with ADOS. I Corps	
"	3/8/18 Sat.		To St Omer to make local purchases	
"	4/8/18 Sun		Usual routine. Demanded 18-pr guns to replace one of B/153 condemned. Received 8 special Vickers A.A. eights.	
"	5/8/18 Mon		To Dunkerque to make local purchases. Received 50 Colt Long and 50 Savage A6 and the Cambridge Auto Anti-Gas for trial.	
"	6/8/18 Tues		Demanded 18-pr gun to replace one of B/123 condemned.	
"	7/8/18 Wed		To Calais to hasten several stores urgently needed by Division.	
"	8/8/18 Thurs		No paint yet arrived at Rouleers but received 1100 Bero Gros out of 3550 Vans. Visited Mins.	

Army Form C. 2118.

WAR DIARY
or
INTELLIGENCE SUMMARY.
(Erase heading not required.)

Instructions regarding War Diaries and Intelligence Summaries are contained in F. S. Regs., Part II. and the Staff Manual respectively. Title pages will be prepared in manuscript.

Place	Date	Hour	Summary of Events and Information	Remarks and references to Appendices
Tordeghem	9/8/18 Friday		In office all morning. Visited Dumps + units in afternoon.	
	10/8/18 Sat.		Railroad Dump, Reinforcement Camps in morning. Office in afternoon.	
	11/8/18 Sun.		His Majesty King George heard at a Special service. It was a good opportunity after the service to meet G.C. O's. etc.	
	12/8/18 Monday		Called on D.D.O.S. II Army & collected various notes for practice purposes.	
	13/8/18 Thurs		Conference in morning of Q.M.s of 108 Bde H&Qr Field very busy wants for Lewis Gunners have written to the Bde Arranged that they to receive of guns extra oil would not be quelous of put in for occasionally	
	14/8/18 Wed		Visited units	
	15/8/18 Thurs		To Dunkirk to make local purchases.	
	16/8/18 Fri.		Usual routine. To dump.	
	17/8/18 Sat.		Visited units.	
	18/8/18 Sund.		Received 6 Tons general stores & H.S. Howitzer gear for 2/173	

Army Form C. 2118.

WAR DIARY
or
INTELLIGENCE SUMMARY.
(Erase heading not required.)

Instructions regarding War Diaries and Intelligence Summaries are contained in F. S. Regs., Part II. and the Staff Manual respectively. Title pages will be prepared in manuscript.

Place	Date	Hour	Summary of Events and Information	Remarks and references to Appendices
Sadghera	19/18	Mon	Vickers barrels urgently required by M.G. Batt. were for same	
"	20/18	Tues	Demanded Lewis Gun for 1st R.I.R. Returned to Gun Park	
"	21/18	Wed	it Lewis Gun Machings not required by division. Received 5th Army Bears but as there were not required by Div Adj. asked for authority to return	
"	22/18	Thurs	Demanded Vickers Gun for F.G. Batt. Artillery fire	
"	23/18	Friday	Received 100 expendable Vickers gun belts.	
"	24/18	Sat	Visited units and ADOS Corps.	
"	25/18	Sun	Received 5 Lewis general stores	
"	26/18	Mon	6 German machine guns (2 heavy - 4 light) received from Corps Workshops. Also, 1 attachment for discharging the .303 rifle grenade for trial and report	
"	27/18	Tues	Demanded 18 ptr gun for B/1/73	

Army Form C. 2118.

WAR DIARY
or
INTELLIGENCE SUMMARY.
(Erase heading not required.)

Instructions regarding War Diaries and Intelligence Summaries are contained in F. S. Regs., Part II. and the Staff Manual respectively. Title pages will be prepared in manuscript.

Place	Date	Hour	Summary of Events and Information	Remarks and references to Appendices
Iseghem	18/9/18	Wed	Usual routine.	
"	19/9/18	Thurs	Demanded 1 Lewis gun, 1.18pr gun and 18-pr carriage to replace others destroyed by shell fire. Took over from 35th division 1 lee auto to re-	
"	20/9/18	Fri	Place a limited number issued to Troops guard.	
"	21/9/18	Sat	Conductor Brennan went on leave and I have charge of Chief clerk of 102nd Bde to office to act as chief clerk during his absence	

18/9/18

[signature]
Major
D.A.P.S.
36 Division

WAR DIARY
or
INTELLIGENCE SUMMARY.

(Erase heading not required.)

Army Form C. 2118.

36th Division

JADS

Place	Date	Hour	Summary of Events and Information	Remarks and references to Appendices
Tezighem	1/9/18 Sun		Office moved to near St Silvestre Cappel. Visited Reception Camp. All serials on move and no stores being drawn.	
St Silvestre Cappel	2/9/18 Mon		Office moved to Mont des Cats and Dump to Godewaersvelde.	
Mont des Cats	3/9/18 Tues		As Dump is at too great a distance from serials, tried to find a suitable dump near to wagon lines, but could find no accommodation nearer than Berthen.	
"	4/9/18 Wed		Moved dump to Berthen. Visited Divl. Reception Camp.	
"	5/9/18 Thurs		To dump and units.	
"	6/9/18 Friday		Office moved to St Jans Cappel. Several demands for S.D. Kitting from Reserve to fit out men who have been gas-shelled. In addition, sent 200 suits to Field Ambulance to meet cases.	

Army Form C. 2118.

WAR DIARY
or
INTELLIGENCE SUMMARY.
(Erase heading not required.)

Place	Date	Hour	Summary of Events and Information	Remarks and references to Appendices
St Jans Cappel	7/9/18 Sat.		Office work interrupted by rain forcing air. Visited units.	
"	8/9/18 Sun.		Went to 1st Army to draw American cloth required for signalling to aeroplanes	
"	9/9/18 Mon.		To camps and several units.	
"	10/9/18 Tues.		To Second Army Troops No 1 at Whatou to draw 1 light and 1 heavy German machine gun for course to 108 Bde.	
"	11/9/18 Wed.		Usual routine. Heavy demands for Lewis Gun parts and mot stores being received.	
"	12/9/18 Thurs.		Usual routine. To dump.	
"	13/9/18 Friday		To dump. Returned German machine guns to Second Army - not now required.	
"	14/9/18 Sat.		Usual routine. Same	
"	15/9/18 Sun.		By car to collect 12" Box respirators special for signalling to aeroplanes to dump.	

WAR DIARY
or
INTELLIGENCE SUMMARY.
(Erase heading not required.)

Army Form C. 2118.

Instructions regarding War Diaries and Intelligence Summaries are contained in F. S. Regs., Part II. and the Staff Manual respectively. Title pages will be prepared in manuscript.

Place	Date	Hour	Summary of Events and Information	Remarks and references to Appendices
St Martin Carpel	16/9/18	Mon	Visited Brigades. 5.D Bales of Blankets arrived at dump and also 488 prs of Gumboots.	
"	17/9/18	Tues	To dump. Issues of first Blankets being made to units.	
"	18/9/18	Wed	To dump and usual routine.	
"	19/9/18	Thurs	By car to new area to fix up billets &c.	
"	20/9/18	Friday	Office moved to Eadale. Camp near St Janviers. Went to D.T. Coy where Second Army to draw H.S. tow	
"	21/9/18	Sat	Began and dump to Hautbergue. Issue from Gum Park to dump. Arranged for stores for 193rd & 76th DFP to be sent out by lorry while this Brigade is temporarily detached.	
"	22/9/18	Sun	Major Mackenzie M.C. proceeded on leave, and Lt Curby took over duties of DADOS during his absence.	

WAR DIARY
or
INTELLIGENCE SUMMARY.

Army Form C. 2118.

(Erase heading not required.)

Place	Date	Hour	Summary of Events and Information	Remarks and references to Appendices
Shar-i-Saya	23/10	Mon	Received four Scout Army Troops at Jacobabad rage and ropes for use at Jacobabad and from Bhadaypur armoured cars for use of spare aeroplanes	
"	24/10	Tue	Still more American cloth required and applications made to ADOS for further supply. Issued bayonet scabbards for use with Jacobabad and sent out Jacobabad to units by lorry.	
"	25/10	Wed	Sent to Dadu american cloth from ADOS I Corps.	
"	26/10	Thu	Collected Jacobabad rake carrying water tins, and carriers ammunition emergency from Corps Troops, also a further supply of American cloth from ADOS I Corps. Sent to Venhevers for 100 bags W.D. for carrying rations. Visited new area to try our new dump.	
Vogelzi	27/10	Friday	Office moved to Vogelzi	
"	28/10	Sat.	Delivered to 152nd Bde F.A. Jacobabad	
"	29/10	Sun.	Dump moved to near Dielen	

Army Form C. 2118.

WAR DIARY
or
INTELLIGENCE SUMMARY.
(Erase heading not required.)

Instructions regarding War Diaries and Intelligence Summaries are contained in F. S. Regs., Part II. and the Staff Manual respectively. Title pages will be prepared in manuscript.

Place	Date	Hour	Summary of Events and Information	Remarks and references to Appendices
Vogelije	30/9/18	Mon	Officer moved to Elverso.	

1/10/18

[signature]
Lt. for Major
D.A.D.O.S.
36 Division

D.A.D.O.S.
36th Div.

Army Form C. 2118.

WAR DIARY
or
INTELLIGENCE SUMMARY.
(Erase heading not required.)

Vol 34

Place	Date	Hour	Summary of Events and Information	Remarks and references to Appendices
Ypres	1/10 Tues		Usual routine.	
	2/10 Wed		Moved office to St Jean.	
St Jean	3/10 Thurs		Received 10000 Lewis spare parts and commenced to issue from spot between St Jean and Ypres where it is proposed to move dump, which is now at too great a distance from units. Also received 3 Lewis guns from fact 18. 7.P.18 and 500 magazines which are to be held as reserve. Dump completed.	
	4/10 Friday		Dump of extra spare parts made.	
	5/10 Sat.		Demanded several Lewis guns for various units.	
	6/10 Sun.		Demanded 10 tin guns & 8 Lewis guns to replace others destroyed. Also 36 Lewis gun bags for Thomas Splints.	
	7/10 Mon		Usual routine	
	8/10 Tues		Sent to Lytham for American cloth.	

WAR DIARY
or
INTELLIGENCE SUMMARY.

(Erase heading not required.)

Army Form C. 2118.

Instructions regarding War Diaries and Intelligence Summaries are contained in F. S. Regs., Part II. and the Staff Manual respectively. Title pages will be prepared in manuscript.

Place	Date	Hour	Summary of Events and Information	Remarks and references to Appendices
St Jean	9th Dec		Received Stewart sleeping members.	
	10th Dec		Received another draft and a glass drawn from	
			Second Army. Trap 96 gas of American cloth.	
	11th Dec	thirty	Lumber clothing issue to units. Twenty	
			Soda Forge indicators collected from I Corps Troops.	
	12th Dec	Sat.	Usual routine.	
	13th Dec	Sun.	Advanced dump, chiefly for purpose of collecting	
			unfit clothing not immediately required by units, closed	
			at Beeclare. Collected from I Corps Troops & Cavalry	
			Corps, 13 anti-gas Vaseline instants.	
	14th Dec	Mon	Sent up anti gas respirators to advanced	
			dump.	
	15th Dec	Tues	Officer and dump moved to near Beeclare	
			is takeover.	
			I arrived & found Division on the move.	
Beeclare	Dec 16		Sent lorries to bring up anti gas stores left at St Jean - Passchendaele line	
			new Railhead. 8 Tons of Stores arrived from Base.	

Army Form C. 2118.

WAR DIARY
or
INTELLIGENCE SUMMARY.
(Erase heading not required.)

Instructions regarding War Diaries and Intelligence Summaries are contained in F. S. Regs., Part II. and the Staff Manual respectively. Title pages will be prepared in manuscript.

Place	Date	Hour	Summary of Events and Information	Remarks and references to Appendices
	1918			
Ledeghem	Oct 17		I moved main Divisional Headqrs to Ledghem — visited dead — 200, 107, 108 & 109 Brigades — arranged for D.R. to take Bulk Indents to Base	
"	" 18		Selected site for Trophy Dump, & also a site for main dump at Hinkel St-Eloi (schools). Visited Becelaere — stopped stores from Base owing to rapid movement forward.	
Hinkle St. Eloi	" 19		Office & Dump from Becelaere moved up to Hinkle St-Eloi — I moved with Divisional H.Qrs to Rondelade	
Rondelade	" 20		Visited Dump & Office at Hinkle St-Eloi, dealt with much accumulated correspondence — stores arrived from Becelaere. About 15 lorry loads to clear near Dumps.	
"	" 21		Went to Corps Headquarters — Stores still coming from Becelaere.	
"	" 22		Idea a meeting of Quartermasters to discuss Ordnance matters. Rail Head changed — now Beythem.	
"	" 23		Took lorry load of Stores & joined to Units at an advanced Refilling Point (B.14. B.7.9 Sheet 29). Visited C.R.E. at Headquarters.	

WAR DIARY
INTELLIGENCE SUMMARY

Army Form C. 2118.

Place	Date	Hour	Summary of Events and Information	Remarks and references to Appendices
	1918			
Londdale	Oct 24		Office + Dump moved to Hulste.	
HULSTE	" 25		Temp Capt/ofmajor C.H. McKenzie admitted to Hospital & transferred to Home establishment.	
"	" 26		Received from base 2000 Blankets, thus completing Blanket Establishment. Return sent to A. D.O.S.	
"	" 27		Nine lorries of Stores arrived.	
"	" 28		Moved dump to LOEWE — office to BELLEGHEM.	
"	"		Railhead changed to HEULE.	
"	"		D.A. D.O.S. met A.+Q.M.G. in New Area	
BELLEGHEM	" 29		Railhead changed to Moorsele. Visited Dump at LOEWE.	
"	"		Called on H.Qrs. 153 Brigade.	
"	"		Took over Improv Account.	
"	" 30		Lorries of Stores arrived at Railhead — visited dump at LOEWE.	
"	"		Drew tools issue for purpose of Pay from Field Cashier	
"	" 31		Paid the men at the Dump. Units drawing Stores very well.	

J.L. Irwin
Lieut
D.A.D.O.S.
36th Division.

Army Form C. 2118.

WAR DIARY
or
INTELLIGENCE SUMMARY.
(Erase heading not required.)

DADOS 36 [?] 9/11/35[?]

Instructions regarding War Diaries and Intelligence Summaries are contained in F. S. Regs., Part II. and the Staff Manual respectively. Title pages will be prepared in manuscript.

Place	Date	Hour	Summary of Events and Information	Remarks and references to Appendices
BELLEGHEM	1918 Nov. 1		Economy in Ordnance Stores G.R.O.s 4773 & 6336 come into force. Went in search of a new Dump at MOUSCRON.	
	" 2		3 Ton General Stores advised. Received very large quantities of Indents. Comparative Return of Burst Issues sent to A.D.O.S.	
	" 3		Visited new Dump at MOUSCRON also old Dump at LOWE. Sent to Railhead (MENIN) for Stores - 2 Vehicles arrived. advised Units to draw.	
MOUSCRON	" 4		Moved Dump & Office to MOUSCRON. Sent Winter Clothing Return to A.D.O.S.	
	" 5		Visited H.Qrs. 107th & 108th Brigades.	
	" 6		" 15 R.I.R. Saw Quartermaster. Received 8 tons of Stores (Rifleing Gear) from Base depot. Major Macaulay [?]late 34 D.O.s) Kit via A.M.F.O.	
	" 7		Nothing unusual occurred.	
	" 8		Stores arrived from Railhead, Sent lorry to Audruicq to collect Stores for Q.	

Army Form C. 2118.

WAR DIARY
or
INTELLIGENCE SUMMARY.
(Erase heading not required.)

Instructions regarding War Diaries and Intelligence Summaries are contained in F. S. Regs., Part II. and the Staff Manual respectively. Title pages will be prepared in manuscript.

Place	Date	Hour	Summary of Events and Information	Remarks and references to Appendices
	1918			
MOUSCRON	Nov 9		Received instructions to move locations for Field Ambulances Divisions, Div Train, Mob. Vet'y Section	
"	" 10		Indented for 2nd Blanket - 10 tons of Stores arrived.	
"	" 11		Nothing unusual occurred.	
"	" 12		Received 4 Tons of Stores from the Base, sent 2 loads of Salvage to Railhead	
"	" 13		Visited A.D.V.S. XV Corps also D.O. XV Corps Troops. Had a good clear up at Dump, Stores surplus to requirements despatched to Railhead.	
"	" 14		2nd Blankets arrived at Railhead. Visited R.T.O. to arrange with him returning of Salvage to Rhead. Sent Stores out to Autreppe & Kaintroy to 3 Corps engineers, Ervoir Inspector & Armourers, to No 3 Field Coys & Pioneers	Met P.M.
"	" 15		Stores arrived from Railhead (Clothing)	
"	" 16		Despatched Stores surplus to requirements to Base - Sent convoy A.E. 13/12/13. -	
"	" 17		Nothing unusual occurred	

Army Form C. 2118.

WAR DIARY
or
INTELLIGENCE SUMMARY.
(Erase heading not required.)

Instructions regarding War Diaries and Intelligence Summaries are contained in F. S. Regs., Part II. and the Staff Manual respectively. Title pages will be prepared in manuscript.

Place	Date	Hour	Summary of Events and Information	Remarks and references to Appendices
MOUSCRON	Nov 18		Visited Railheads also visited H.Q 109th Brigade. Sent Monthly Clothing Return to A.D.O.S.	
"	19		Nothing of unusual occurrence.	
"	20		Received 3 Ton of Stores at Railhead. Sent 4 Armourers to 107 Bde to rebond Rifles, machine guns etc. Salvaged Armourer with Reserve Line Camp to return.	
"	21		Sisters arrived at Railhead (Clothing) changed from 3rd to 15th Corps.	
"	22		Sent Lorry to collect Stout pipes for R.E. Lorries also went to collect Stores from Divisional Dump to be returned to Base.	
"	23		6500 Parcels received from Base. Sent 4 lorry loads Salvage to Railhead. S/Sergt. Dedcown reported for duty.	
"	24		Sent Surplus Stores to Railhead for despatch to Base. A.D.O.S. XV Corps visited this Dump.	
"	25		4 Armourers Sent to 107 Bde returned after completion of duty.	
"	26		Paid the men. Minister Blessing Reported Sick to A.D.M.S. Demanded 1. 4. 5" How: for D/153 Bde condemned by I.O.M.	

Army Form C. 2118.

WAR DIARY
or
INTELLIGENCE SUMMARY.

(Erase heading not required.)

Instructions regarding War Diaries and Intelligence Summaries are contained in F. S. Regs., Part II. and the Staff Manual respectively. Title pages will be prepared in manuscript.

Place	Date	Hour	Summary of Events and Information	Remarks and references to Appendices
Thouroun	Nov. 27		4 Armourers sent to 108 Bde. to overhaul Rifles, Machine Guns etc. Day of best Indents charged - units advised. Rhum Rations issued.	
"	28		Lewis Guns now relieved - Others arrived but very late. 2 Armourers sent to 109 Brigade for tour of units. S/Cond. Trevenna returning from leave to U.K.	
"	29		Issued soap to Bains as an urgent case - Issued 51 day sup. dump so administered by No. 5 Gun Park for Gun Park Stores - 96.5 - Stores arrived. Called on H.Q. 109 Bde.	
"	30		Visited No. 5 Gun Park. Sent return of weekly Tonnage etc. to A.D.O.S. - Stores arrived from D.A.R.C.(Division)	

Head Qrs.

30. Nov. 1918

H. Henri
Major
D.A.D.O.S. 36th Divn.

Army Form C. 2118.

Tabor.
36th Divn.

WAR DIARY
or
INTELLIGENCE SUMMARY.
(Erase heading not required.)

Instructions regarding War Diaries and Intelligence Summaries are contained in F. S. Regs., Part II. and the Staff Manual respectively. Title pages will be prepared in manuscript.

Place	Date	Hour	Summary of Events and Information	Remarks and references to Appendices
MOUSE ROAD	1918 Dec 1		100 camp FS arrived for distribution. Well between to the S/Byg. (Sunday.)	
"	2		4 Armourers arrived from D.H.G. wis 10 B Base, 2 have been sent to log bag, making 4 to complete overhauling of guns & rifles.	
"	3		Sent 2 Lorries to Remp. under indications of QM Branch. Sent 2 Lorries to Reception Camp to put up 1000 Blankets & leave at Baths to be disinfected. Attended lecture on show we won the great War.- Received a quantity of Horse Respirators for return to Base.	
"	4		Ins[pect]ion of Stores advised, inspected Shoemakers Shop & Armourers Shop	
"	5		2 Armourers reporting respective to 153 Bde, 173 Bde & DAC for Tour of duty. - 96 Boxes horseshoes arrived from Base.	
"	6		Visited Baiza - 1180 Horse Rugs advised - spoke to ADOS on Elephant re vehicles if available in Army etc. Horse Rum Ration at 6 p.m.	
"	7		Visited HeadQrs R.A. nil returns sent to A.D.S. nothing of unusual occurrence.	
"	8		Visited R.O.O. at Coimbra, tried to get Binoculars Prismatic. No Stores arrived, no item to-day. Coriscillo Branch applied FCA.	

A6915 Wt. W14422/M1160 330,000 12/16. D. D. & L. Forms/C./2118/14.

Army Form C. 2118.

WAR DIARY
or
INTELLIGENCE SUMMARY.
(Erase heading not required.)

Instructions regarding War Diaries and Intelligence Summaries are contained in F. S. Regs., Part II. and the Staff Manual respectively. Title pages will be prepared in manuscript.

Place	Date	Hour	Summary of Events and Information	Remarks and references to Appendices
	1918			
MOUSCRON	Dec 9		Wires arrived from Railhead. Drew 100 trousers from B.O.S. Canteen funds for Christmas	
"	10		Drew per M.T. men from field cashier. Sent 4 lorries to Marcoin en Perenin to draw stores dumped there under Army instructions. A.D.O.S & Capt Burrard called.	
"	11		1 No SSN RAOC received special corps orders issued by Major Gen. Parsons congratulating Corps on all done during late Somme Retirement. Stores received from Base.	
"	12		Nothing of unusual occurrence	
"	13		Attended conference in A.D.O.S. Office, Roubaix. Vehicles arrived at Railhead	
"	14		Sent away Reserves of B.M. Respirators. Stores (necessaries) arrived ex Railhead. 6 Bicycles received by D.A.P.M. from civilians sent into Ord Store.	
"	15		No 1 Section No 2 Army Workshops Coy R.E. attached for ordnance stores.	

Army Form C. 2118.

WAR DIARY
or
INTELLIGENCE SUMMARY.
(Erase heading not required.)

Instructions regarding War Diaries and Intelligence Summaries are contained in F. S. Regs., Part II. and the Staff Manual respectively. Title pages will be prepared in manuscript.

Place	Date	Hour	Summary of Events and Information	Remarks and references to Appendices
	1918			
MOUSCRON	Dec 16		3rd Blanket arrived under A.R.O. 3399. H.M.E.s Blessing. Return to A.D.O. Chief Clerk away sick.	
			Visited Staff Capt. 36th Div. Arty.	
	17		Visit to corps dump which I have taken over at Courtrai. Stores arrived Railhead. 3rd Blanket wire pr (6000) also R.O.O. Ironacum	
"	18		Visited Staff Capt. 108 Bde - also R.O.O. Ironacum	
"	19		Nothing unusual occurred.	
"	20		Stores arrived at Railhead, visited & inspected Shoemakers & Armourer's shop.	
"	21		Return Ration Strength to Q. Tonnage etc to A Som.	
"	22		Staff went to an Ordnance Conference at Corps, proceeded by a Ten.	
"	23		Stores arrived - visited Condition XIX Corps Dump	
"	24		Paid men - 3rd Blanket arrived at Railhead - A Som. Cancel - Dates of Buck Indents changed to schedule B.	
"	25		Christmas Day - a holiday granted to the Staff.	

Army Form C. 2118.

WAR DIARY
or
INTELLIGENCE SUMMARY.
(Erase heading not required.)

Instructions regarding War Diaries and Intelligence Summaries are contained in F. S. Regs., Part II. and the Staff Manual respectively. Title pages will be prepared in manuscript.

Place	Date	Hour	Summary of Events and Information	Remarks and references to Appendices
MOUSCRON	1918 Dec 26		Visited other showrooms shop. Sent Salah; Relief, transport & V.L. Conf.	
"	27		Major F.L. HUTH, enjoyed on leave to 10/1/19. Sent L.P. return to B.9.9.d.	
"	28		6 Tons stores advised, new South demand scheme came into use	
"	29		2d S.Sgt Hatter promoted to 6 weeks Kingsgrove leave	
"	30		nothing unusual ordinary routine work going on	
"	31		ditto	

J.A. Moyes Lieut
Infantry
O.C. D.A.D. 36.B. Divn

WAR DIARY
or
INTELLIGENCE SUMMARY.
(Erase heading not required.)

Army Form C. 2118.

D.A.D.S.T. 36th Div. Vol 37

Instructions regarding War Diaries and Intelligence Summaries are contained in F. S. Regs., Part II. and the Staff Manual respectively. Title pages will be prepared in manuscript.

Place	Date	Hour	Summary of Events and Information	Remarks and references to Appendices
Maroeuil	1919 Jany 1st		2 Tons Stores admired. Demanded 3, 18 pdr firings A.T. 13 Bde R.F.A. & 1 for B. 153 Bde R.F.A and ordinary rail line with going on. Q.S.S. stores to R.H.	
"	2nd		Nothing unusual, ordinary rail line.	
"	3rd		Demanded 60 steel Q.M. Huts. Fifth A.R.O. 2nd list of 29/1/19 by order of A.D.S.	
"	3rd		2 tons Stores admired and 2 Tons stores received	
"	4th		Sent 3 lorry loads of salvage Clothing & Leather Stores & saddlers for B&O whs	
"	5th		1 lorry to Lestroi for urgent work. No base train running to day	
"	5th		Railhead changed from Anzin to Moncecroux. Demanded 1 x 18" Wheel	
"	6th		and carriage for B.173 Bde R.F.A. 4 Tons Lewis Stores admired.	
"	6th		Lt. Hague R.I.R. went on leave & Lieut N. Bannerman R.F.A. H.Q. took over A.Q.S.T. XV Corps	
"	7th		Visited dump.	
"	8th		Miss Lena Ashwells Concert Party gave performance in Collège Lt. Hague rest. from leave	
"	8th		— ditto — 6 carts allotted to D.A.D.S. 5 ton stores admired and 237 soldiers	
"	9th		Demanded 1, 18 pdr firings for A. 173 from 15 S. Corps Troops	
"	10th		Lt. Cowlbaith visited 18 Divis King's Coy. 5 tons stores admired	
"	11th		Lt. Hague returned to England for Demobilization	
"	12th		3 Tons stores admired. D.A.D.O. returned from leave.	

WAR DIARY
or
INTELLIGENCE SUMMARY.

(Erase heading not required.)

Army Form C. 2118.

Place	Date	Hour	Summary of Events and Information	Remarks and references to Appendices
MOUSCRON	1919 Jan 13		A/173 Bde advised to draw 1 18-Pdr from No 5 Gun Park.	
	14		Stores received from Base.	
			Washed Boots Ankles & Leather from Base — A.D.O.S carried also O.O. X.E.A. to whom clothing was invoiced.	
"	15		Visited Staff Capt. 109 Bde. at RONCQUE. also O X 3 Dominion.	
			Railhead at MENIN. Indented for 1 & 5-How. for D/173 Bde.	
"	16		Nothing of unusual occurred.	
	17		Stores arrived at Railhead. Pilfering still going on.	
			Visited Quartermaster Stores of 15th & 15th Batt. R. Irish Rifles.	
	18		Usual weekly Returns despatched. Bulk wine despatched.	
	19		4 Tons General Stores arrived. Railhead. half holiday	
			& the Staff as normal on Sundays.	
	20		A.D.O.S Corps called. Lieut Simmons. Assist-Inspector of Armourers I Army reported for tour of duty.	
			Visited Q.M. Stores 16th R. Irish Rifles.—	
	21		Nothing of unusual occurred	

WAR DIARY
or
INTELLIGENCE SUMMARY.
(Erase heading not required.)

Army Form C. 2118.

Place	Date	Hour	Summary of Events and Information	Remarks and references to Appendices
MOUSCRON	22		Visited A.D.O.S. XV Corps. Hastened stores from Base.	
"	23		Visited Staff Capt. 107th Bde.	
			Hired A.D.O.S. position as regards Boots Ankle	
			Visited 10 B Bde, & saw Staff Capt.	
"	24		Writing of unusual occurrence report.	
"	25		Indented for Ammun. Major Q.F. 18 Pdr. for A/173 Bde to replace one condemned. Received stores from Base. Sent weekly return.	
"	26		Received Boots clothing from Base. - 2 Travels arrived R'hove. Indented for 1 Q.F. 18 Pdr. Can. for B/173 to replace condemned.	
"	27		Visited Railhead - Sent 2 Lony loads of salvage clothing & equipment. Stock R'hove for despatch to Base. Visited Brown Bars.	
"	28		Received 300 pair of Boots as a result of arrangement with Corps - Indented for 1000 Camp details for dismounted horses.	
"	29		A/A.D.O.S. carried forward sack clothing to them for making up cut rations for field Punishment Compound.	

Army Form C. 2118.

WAR DIARY
or
INTELLIGENCE SUMMARY.
(Erase heading not required.)

Instructions regarding War Diaries and Intelligence Summaries are contained in F. S. Regs., Part II, and the Staff Manual respectively. Title pages will be prepared in manuscript.

Place	Date	Hour	Summary of Events and Information	Remarks and references to Appendices
	1919			
MOUSCRON	Jan 30		Received Q.F. 18-Pdr. 179.6 off my Instant 1315	
			Q.F. Mod carriage 1036 — 1017	
		"	Q.F. " 4.5" 3576 — 1318	
		"	Q.F. 18-Pdr " 441 1323	
		"	Q.F. 4.5" How 605 1322	
		"	Q.F. 4.5" " 3073 1309	
MOUSCRON	"	31	Received "Thaw Precautions" order. Lorries returned to M.T. Coy.	
			Harbored equipment for 36th Div Ammun Col.	
			J.L. Irwin	
			Major	
			O.A.S.O.R. 36th Div Ammun	
			January 1919	

WAR DIARY or INTELLIGENCE SUMMARY

Army Form C. 2118.

DADOS 36ᵗʰ Divⁿ
Vol 36

Place	Date	Hour	Summary of Events and Information	Remarks and references to Appendices
MOUSERON	1919 Feb 1		Received Ammon. Wagon & Limber No 18935 off my Indent 1307 also 18-Pdr Cam No 15796 off my Indent 1338. Pit to be returned from Leave. Ration Return sent to Div H.Q. Tonnage Return to A.S.C.	
"	2		Visited Artillery Q.M. Stores round Tunering. Sent report to "Q" Branch on Economy in Ordnance Stores asked for. Selected site for Intermediate Corrective Station under Corps Order No 906. Seven Lorries of Stores advised from Base.	
"	3		7 Tons of Stores arrived. Arranged with "Q" Branch for Transport. Issued Rhum. Lt. Draper arrived for tour of duty with Division.	
"	4		Paid the Staff unusual fortnightly Payment. Initial Staff Capt. 107 Bde. & 2 R.G. Rifles Q.M. Stores.	
"	5		Hired M/17/3 Roll to draw from Gun Park 1 wagon Limm. R.F. 18-Pdr. Visited 16ᵗʰ R.Irish Rifles Q.M. Stores. Sergt. Shaw reported sick.	
"	6		Nothing of unusual occurrence.	

WAR DIARY
or
INTELLIGENCE SUMMARY.
(Erase heading not required.)

Army Form C. 2118.

Place	Date	Hour	Summary of Events and Information	Remarks and references to Appendices
MOUSCRON	1919 Feb 7		Stores arrived from Base, but unable to get at them until to-morrow. Arranged with A.D.O.S for 200 pair of Boots urgently required.	
"	" 8		Usual weekly Returns submitted. D.D.O.S. 2nd Army expected but yet arrived. 72 Denim suits undergoing repairs, a modification to pinson casings done during west winter to day.	
"	9		Morning of unusual occurrence to report.	
"	10		5m.5m Stores arrived. 4/A.S.O.S. exped.	
"	11		700 Pair Boots arrived. Hastened 60 Overalls from Base	
"	12		Fetched 100 Pair of Boots from O.O. Corps Troops A. General Rhinn Ration to 2m man.	
"	13		1000 Hurlin Specimens demanded received, 2 A.D.O.S. arrived.	
"	14		Morning of unusual occurrence to report	
"	15		2 men for Salvage work arrived, 3bm of stores advised. Usual weekly Return despatched. Sent 8 Lorry loads of Salvage to New dump for Storage.	

WAR DIARY
or
INTELLIGENCE SUMMARY

Army Form C. 2118.

(Erase heading not required.)

Place	Date	Hour	Summary of Events and Information	Remarks and references to Appendices
MOUSCRON	Feb 16 1919		3 Tons of Equipment Stores arrived at Rail Head, a further 3 tons of Stores advised. C/Capt. Enough put in application for 3 days leave to Brussels.	
"	17		Four lorries ordered to report to our ordnance annexe. Received Clothing Returns enveloped from ordnance. Received an application from 2 Can. Bn. Q.F. 18 Pdr. also 1 Can. Tol. Q.F. 18 Pdr.	
"	18		6 Tons Clothing arrived. Visited a site for Stores on demobilization with Major Rogers. Rains new. 2 men arrived for duty with Salvage.	
"	19		Nothing of unusual importance occurred.	
"	20		A.D.O.S. called & visited I.C.S (unit Armourials sources) (Calais). 9 units A.P.O. in the morning. Visited Sunday Service. Stores (Hosiery sports) arrived from Ostend. Visited Q.M. 1st Army at Baron Trophy.	
"	21		Application from lorries to return sent to Bases of Salvage. & I.C.S for Stores - Stores from Calais A.D.O.S. Telephoned re machine carts. Re-Selecting leather fastenings & Loops in Bundles of 10.	

A6945 Wt W14422/M1160 35,000 12/16 D.D. & L. Forms/C/2118/74.

WAR DIARY
or
INTELLIGENCE SUMMARY.
(Erase heading not required.)

Army Form C. 2118.

Instructions regarding War Diaries and Intelligence Summaries are contained in F.S. Regs., Part II. and the Staff Manual respectively. Title pages will be prepared in manuscript.

Place	Date	Hour	Summary of Events and Information	Remarks and references to Appendices
MOUSCRON	1918			
	Feb 22		Visited I.C.S. & made arrangements about getting away salvage – 11 Tons of Stores arrived – Belais open to receive salvage at the rate of 1 Truck load per diem.	
	23		Stores arrived from Roubaix – Visited 12 Royal Iris h Rifles, saw new draft on Parade, clothing very bad, as this Unit is for the Army of occupation every endeavour is being made to equip them.	
	24		Brig. Gen. Vaughan called. D.D.S. called with A.D.O.S.	
	25		Blouins arrived from Roubaix – Went with Party of 44 men to Corps Newton's (10th) funeral. Sent Truck of Salvage to Base.	
	26		Visited New Dumps. depeleted of 1 Truck Salvage to Base. Received quantity of Valuable Stores being handed in by Units.	
	27		Received 6 Lorry loads of Surplus Stores from XV Corps Troops Reception Camp.	
	28		Went to town with Fifth Army to learn his breegers. Sent Blankets to I.O.S. for Storage. Stores arrived from Roubaix – 1 Lorry Load.	

F.L. Hinton
Major
Senior 36 Division

WAR DIARY or INTELLIGENCE SUMMARY

Army Form C. 2118.

DARTS 36R

MAY

Place	Date	Hour	Summary of Events and Information	Remarks and references to Appendices
MOUSCRON	1/5/19		Cadres reduced and 4 Officers and 274 other ranks sent for demobilisation. Major General Ford D.Q.M.G. Northern Troops France & Flanders held a conference which we attended & Lt Col Crawford (who the Division was supporting) Craig Prisple here & 107 Regs representing D.A.P.G. M.G. matters to Cadres as was divisional.	
	9			
	10			
	11			
	12			
	13			
	14			
	15			
	16			
	17			
	18			
	19			
	20			
	21		Lt Col Hunt Comdt 15th R.I. Rifles proceeded to command 43rd Labour Group.	
	22		Cadre of 2nd R. Innis. Fus. left for U.K. Lt Col Crawford DSO in command.	
	23		Cadre of 15th R. Irish Rifles left for U.K. Lt Col Hayes Anderson h.c. in command.	
	26			
	27			
	28			
	29			
	30		Major Howard O.C. 36th Signal Coy left for demobilisation	
	31			

www.ingramcontent.com/pod-product-compliance
Lightning Source LLC
Chambersburg PA
CBHW080905230426
43664CB00016B/2733